THE GOLDEN LAWS OF ENLIGHTENMENT

MASTER NICK EAGLE

The Golden Laws of Enlightenment
Published by: Eagle Vortex
Arizona, AZ

EAGLE, NICK, DR.
MASTER NICK EAGLE

Library of Congress Control Number: 2025917603
ISBN: 979-8-9998291-0-8, 979-8-9998291-2-2 (Paperback)
ISBN: 979-8-9998291-1-5, 979-8-9998291-3-9 (Hardcover)

BODY, MIND & SPIRIT / Healing / Prayer & Spiritual
PHILOSOPHY / Metaphysics
SELF-HELP / Meditations

QUANTITY PURCHASES: Schools, companies, professional groups, clubs, and other organizations may qualify for special terms when ordering quantities of this title.

For information, email eagleawakenme@gmail.com

I respond to all brief and respectful messages sent to me on social media, and I offer paid email responses and video chats (Awakening Sessions) for more of my time and energy to have a deeper conversation.
I will gift you an Awakening Session if you send me a screenshot of an Amazon five-star review:
EMAIL: eagleawakenme@gmail.com

WEBSITES/SOCIAL MEDIA:
nickeaglemystic.com eaglevortex.com

TABLE OF CONTENTS

AWAKENING SESSION NOTES

AWAKENING SESSION NOTES

FOREWORD: BE A MYSTIC

How many signs does one need before becoming a knower?
- Master Nick Eagle

I was going to release this book after my first full chakra Kundalini awakening, again after my greatest awakening, and then after completing my PhD in Philosophy. Still, I waited until the time was right. Until I spent many more days with my thoughts, building Eagle Vortex and digesting all that had happened. I continued to apply my teachings and gain even more knowledge and power to find the best words. As I go back through this book, I delete so much. I am rewriting everything again. Words are overrated and overused. They are reasonably necessary in many situations, but most struggle to find them, as they pretend the more they speak, the more they teach, and most just repeat what others have once said, as truth and power get lost. The words have now been found. Knowledge does not come from reading and memorizing words.

I no longer remember who said what; I remember the lessons. I no longer learn from books. I enjoy reading original and creative works, but I now have access to all I seek.

To become a master teacher and healer, we must not only put in the effort to figure out what we are, but also master ourselves, master confidence and find the words to help others. True knowledge is not found in any book; it is found within. I started this book long ago, knowing I would be prepared and ready to release it one day. It is that day, March 16th, 2025. Two days after spending over 30 minutes wrapped in a wet sheet, in temperatures below 16 degrees with 25 miles per hour winds. Two days after my final initiation into shamanism. The same week, I first shared with the world a full chakra opening meditation as I created a spinning Merkaba light vessel, also known as a rainbow light body, for all to see. I have now become a master yogi and a master shaman without anyone else showing me the way. All those who attempted failed me. "God" showed me. I showed myself by "listening" and by being. I will teach you how to listen and be. I will teach you how to become your teacher. It is time for me to teach you what we are. It is time to leave behind weak beliefs and put in the effort to know. It is time to be spiritual. It is time to be a mystic. It is time to seek divine experiences and sacred practices to leave behind fear and suffering. It is time to wake up...if you so choose.

I ask that you do not explore or read my old book. Although it holds much truth, was an excellent guide, and has advanced teachings that led me here, it is basic compared to this book, and I do not approve of all of its energy. All the teachings in it are also present in this book, and they are more fully developed. Do not skip around with this book; it appropriately tells a story and prepares you. If read in the search of truth, it is guaranteed to awaken you on some level, and it will help induce very powerful awakenings in those who decide to be ready. I highly recommend deciding to be ready. I'm not having anyone edit this book. I do not want any outside energy or influence to enter it, and this is a great lesson to begin with. These are very advanced and sacred teachings given to me because I was worthy and prepared. I must be cautious about whom I share this with. Writing such a book for anyone to access is a huge responsibility. If you ever need me, I am here to serve those who bring the right energy, gratitude and appreciation for the work and effort I have put in. I hope to see you at my home, Eagle Vortex Awakening Sanctuary, in Sedona, Arizona, someday.

I DEMAND YOU TAKE THIS SACRED OATH BEFORE YOU PROCEED

By reading this book, you agree to have only the highest level of respect and appreciation for my words and the energy and effort that went into this creation. You also agree to read it with an open mind in a search for truth, knowing it will be your first time hearing many of these teachings, as much of the world that lives in darkness chooses not to be ready for. By reading this book and consciously applying my methods, you are taking responsibility for your thoughts, actions and outcomes. You hold me, Master Nick Eagle, harmless from any results, effects, side effects or coincidences that result from reading, and you release me from any liability for your actions. You agree to only share this sacred knowledge with those who are deserving and have the highest level of respect for us and it. Reading this book and simply having me in your thoughts will always provide you with much protection. Satnam.

GRATITUDE & APPRECIATION

Gratitude and appreciation are how we should start every day, and this is how I'm going to start my book. Please take a moment to take a couple of deep breaths in through the nose and give thanks for the beautiful life that has been gifted to you and for this book that took much effort and energy to create. If somebody does not have the highest level of gratitude and appreciation for creation or my energy, they will not be a part of my life. You must learn the importance of this. This is what is rooted in the Golden Laws of Enlightenment.

Having much gratitude and appreciation is an excellent lesson for peace and power. You must learn what you are so you know that whatever life brings your way, not only can you handle it, but understand it is also a gift. Everything is a challenge, an opportunity and an experience that makes it so special.

IT IS OKAY TO NOT KNOW

When we enter this world, we know nothing, yet we have access to everything. We are only separated by guidance that allows us to connect, heal and obtain answers, or disconnect, harm and live in fear and distraction. Not knowing things does not make you a fool. Lying and pretending to know things is foolish because it brings and feeds darkness and prevents development and awakenings.

I would rather be friends with someone who doesn't know anything and isn't afraid to learn and seek truth rather than someone who pretends to have answers. If there is ANY "ego" or fear attached to your teachings, everything you teach is a lie. I've read and witnessed very few who should even attempt to teach about awakening and attaining Enlightenment. Many hold some lessons and secrets, but few have ever put it all together. And the slightest hint of fear poisons everything that you say.

MY FIRST AWAKENING

"You will not get anywhere if you lie about where you came from."
- Master Nick Eagle

It began when I moved to California after my four-year tour with the Air Force and finished my bachelor's degrees in English and Journalism. It was time to step into my power, pursue entertainment, and admit I was a fool for choosing distraction and fear so I could achieve some success. From a book, I read the quote, "Whenever the devil knocks on the door of my heart, Jesus answers and tells him there is no room." I lost it. I never knew words could have such power. This was my first awakening. Something broke. It was not painful; it was beautiful. I cried tears of ecstasy, joy and acceptance. I took responsibility for every poor decision I had ever made and all the darkness I had brought to the world. It was me. It was not because of my parents, "mental disorders," or anything else external to myself. I never had to pretend. I never had to lie. I could've put in more effort. I could've spent my time more wisely. I could've looked in the right places. Flashes of all the times I lied, was impatient, angry and conjured darkness flew before my eyes. I cried for hours and it felt so good. I never felt such relief through understanding. I decided to stop fighting with "God." From that day forward, I vowed to leave behind all fear and seek truth. I knew I had to operate at my full potential to do so, and it was time to figure out how to achieve it.

WAKE UP MORE

"Do not seek acceptance from a world that should not be accepted."
- Master Nick Eagle

Wake up more and more and more. Never be content; be fulfilled knowing there is more, as you seek it. Seek and you will find. This is purpose. This is the challenge from being born with all the knowledge to figuring out how to access it. Crave it. Understand that the more effort you put in and the more knowledge you have, the less you, AKA the world, will suffer.

See all of the good but do not fear seeing the bad, much less confronting it. Get to the point where you can call it out and laugh at it as it pretends to have power. Understand it. It is pretending, lies, ignorance and nonsense. We only suffer because we choose darkness. Glow as bright as it takes to remove ALL of the darkness you put inside of you. We will not forget the darkness; we will respect it, and we will acknowledge that it is necessary, but it no longer serves us.

Much of this world has been created to make you weak and make money off of you and darkness does not only take your money. School systems are designed to sedate you and have you obey, as they fill you with nonsense that doesn't leave any room for finding truth and answers. Colleges indoctrinate you and force ideologies to serve darkness. Most religions are businesses that dare teach you to fear this manmade "God," as they pretend you are nothing without them. Deep down, you know there isn't one sin one must have ever done or one that one must ever do. Perhaps if we stop turning away from those who choose to, they can be taught better ways. We were all born perfect and in the image of "God." How dare one pretend "God" makes mistakes. Much of the American spiritual community teaches you that you are filled with all this trauma and darkness, and they feed it, "comfort" you, and take your money. Western "medicine" profits from your sickness. Modern Psychology, the DSM-5, and the pharmaceutical industry teach that you are not responsible for your creation; you are broken, incapable and cannot heal yourselves.

We are still monkeys. We are a zero-level civilization. We need about 1% of us to become enlightened to have enough to stand up to evil and take us out of the darkness. One day, we will not be driven by greed. One day, nobody will starve. One day, we will calculate that lying to and taking advantage of our brothers and sisters is so foolish and that there is nothing to gain. This is the great awakening. We all feel it. We all know it. The truth is here. We have never accelerated so quickly. Join those who choose to accelerate or be left in the dark.

So few of this world want you all capable and all-powerful because they will not be able to control you or make money off of you. They fear your power. You need to set aside everything you have been taught and are unsure of. Do not trust anything until you can discover truth on your own. I will tell you the truth and teach you how to find it because it will not matter to your life until you do. It is time to leave this pretend world of greed, sickness and suffering behind.

OPERATE AT YOUR FULL POTENTIAL & BE CONFIDENT

"If we failed you, you do not fail you."
– Master Nick Eagle

The more intelligent we become, the more advanced and enlightened we are. Intelligent beings have a high level of appreciation and love, making them highly vibrational. Super advanced civilizations do not need weapons, police, and military because the lessons have been taught. New civilizations need them for protection from people who do not yet understand how foolish it is to steal from or harm one of their brothers or sisters. Advanced beings possess IQs and calculating abilities that are many times greater than those of the average human. The more intelligent we become, the more we understand and the less we suffer. All that suffering and destruction is all you and it does not have to be.

My last book was a guide to gaining confidence and reaching your full potential. I now consider the tone and much of my word choice quite basic and unevolved, yet a lot of it does make me proud. I am disappointed that I used the "f-word" at all, much less the many times that I did. It was an attempt to shock you, get your attention and make you strong. I now see that as foolish and understand how low vibrational and destructive that word is. That word carries much darkness and after my greatest awakening, you will soon hear much about, it left my vocabulary.

Although it was many moons, and as it seems, many lifetimes ago since I wrote that book, I am very impressed of the truth that I had the strength to discover and write. And I am mostly impressed by the title. Operating at your full potential and being confident are the two most significant factors on the path to enlightenment and purpose. Little did I know that this guide would lead me here, but now this book will be an even more effective guide. My Metaphysics master's thesis explored the importance of having confidence in order to begin the journey of self-discovery and mastery.

MASTERING CONFIDENCE IS THE BEGINNING OF THE SPIRITUAL JOURNEY

"You are exactly what you are supposed to be, unless you realize what you are." - Master Nick Eagle

I began writing my Master's thesis on the importance of confidence in the spiritual journey and it allowed me to realize that it is everything to start it. Little did I know, when I began this journey of mastering confidence and even wrote my book on it, that this is where it would take me. After you learn what we are and what we are capable of, this is where you end up. This is where we will all end up. If you're not connected to and haven't found your "soul," you're not a "spiritual" being. Most of us live in fear and distraction, do not seek personal growth, and never have a chance to be in touch with our souls. The day you step out of the darkness and see everything as not scary but an opportunity to learn and grow, guess what happens? The best yoga practice for spiritual growth is to be honest about what you are and open to new beginnings.

After an interview with a magazine, the magazine labeled me as "Confidence Man." It was the first time I stepped into my power and owned what I was capable of. Most of my life was spent hiding, shaking and pretending I wasn't deciding to be such a weak and incapable fool. I pretended to be broken for much of my life and had to fake confidence to appear confident. I knew the importance of it. I knew it was something we all had to discover to get anywhere. And I knew faking it never did anything. It is beyond foolish even to suggest you cannot be confident if you have never been.

I always knew that I had to face my fears to get past them. I would see other confident people and I KNEW DEEP DOWN that I could be like that; I just had to figure out how. I knew I had to make better decisions, such as what I put into my body, to give myself the best chance. I knew I had to seize the moment and take advantage of the opportunities. I KNEW I HAD TO PUT IN MORE EFFORT. I remember staring at a girl I wanted to talk to many times, but never doing so. And now, to this day, I immediately approach and start a conversation with every person I see who looks interesting.

I was a "pick-up coach" for a few years and spoke at the "World Pick-Up Artist Summit." I was one of the few who taught young men to master their confidence instead of trying to trick girls. My early years were spent doing that, and I never once tricked anyone; only some pretended with me.

A big part of being confident is what you "bring to the table." You must master truth, AKA, being genuine. You must vibrate high and be witty, charming and funny. You must have a story. You must have stuff to talk about. You must have things that you are passionate about. You must learn instruments and have songs to offer. You must have teachings. You must pull it all together and never stop until you do. You must be open to improvement and KNOW DEEP DOWN that you can improve. It's time to put in effort and leave behind the pretending that you are incapable. Get out of your way and move forward.

My counseling sessions and in-person healing and guidance bookings began as confidence coaching, and they have evolved to be so much more; however, the root of all of them remains the mastery of confidence. You will never know or meet your true self if you do not. You will never experience significant personal growth, evolution, or ascension, and you have no business considering parenting a child if you have not become confident. Do you really want your child to be like you? And you will most definitely never have a major awakening. Do everything you can to gain confidence.

BE A WARRIOR

"You must become a warrior to become a protector."
- Master Nick Eagle

There is no choice. You MUST learn how to defend and protect; until you do, you will never be confident and will never learn the basics of what you are. I am a Brazilian jiu-jitsu world champion and black belt. I have studied every form of self-defense, and there isn't a person on the planet I couldn't handle myself with, but there isn't one person on the planet I would ever want to fight.

There is nothing more foolish than fighting anyone, including those who are small. You never know if they have a knife, weapon or allies close by, and if you "win" a fight, you most likely damage your hands and you might get charged or sued as well. Fighting is always a last resort and should be avoided whenever possible. I haven't been in a fight since I was a teenager and I stand up to darkness almost every day.

An intelligent warrior will be able to communicate that they are not someone that anyone would ever want to fight, and a darkness fighter will always stand up to disrespect and never allow it to get away with lying or taking power from you with words.

No woman on the planet should ever provoke or challenge a man, and they should have pepper spray close by at all times. And when you think you may have to use it, you have it out, aimed and ready. If the man does not listen or gets too close, you unload the entire spray into their eyes until it stops spraying. I am also okay with guns, in the hands of those who have been properly trained. This world will need them until everyone wakes up. You should never carry fear and you should always be aware.

DO NOT FEAR AWAKENING

"One who fears their power will never use it."
- Master Nick Eagle

It is beyond dark and twisted for one to suggest that awakening can be scary or that one can "go insane." "The dark night of the soul" is happening now if you have not been awakened and you are in hell being tortured as you read. You do not know better. You become accustomed to fear and a lack of understanding. You hide and distract yourself. How dare a dark sorcerer attempt to intimidate and scare you from awakening and releasing kundalini energy that will allow you to connect, obtain answers and heal. Releasing kundalini energy has never hurt a soul. Only those who run from "God" choose fear and sedation hurt themselves. Darkness and fear are conjured from disconnecting, NOT CONNECTING. Do not allow these people to gain power over you and scare you into thinking some people can not handle doing so, or that one is "not ready." Not ready to not suffer? Not ready to learn and understand things, feel good and enjoy life?? You should be scared of not being scared??

BE AN EAGLE

"Instead of proving what you are, prove what you can be."
– Master Nick Eagle

I am sure many of you have noticed my name change from Nick Hawk to Nick Eagle. After leaving my very lucrative life and Las Vegas behind, I also decided to leave my old name behind. We must lose all attachment to energies that no longer serve us and an upgraded name is a great way to evolve into a new being. I am not trying to hide from my old life. I embrace it as much as one could; it made me this. If I were hiding from it, I would have chosen a new first name and maybe not the last name of another bird and the bird would not have chosen me.

The hawk connects to higher realms with great spiritual awareness and is a protector, but the eagle represents truth, freedom, power, and immortality. It is a much better representation of me and my Awakening Sanctuary. I am no longer watching and studying this world while protecting us; I am now ferociously going after all darkness and all lies, and they no longer have any chance.

BE REFRESHING

Can you think of a better compliment than "refreshing?" It means "serving to refresh." This is precisely what I do. I want to freshen you up and have you step away from the darkness and be reborn into the light. Everything we do should, including compliments, should be refreshing. One that shows honest gratitude and appreciation, as opposed to a desperate attempt to get someone's energy by either lying or telling a truth they are well aware of. Someone once said I have great stature and I was good with it. I will accept original ones. Most attempts to gain my energy are weak. "How are you?" How dare you suggest I would choose to be anything but amazing and have great appreciation for this day? "You look good." I am well aware I look good; I take immaculate care of myself and I put much effort and consideration into my appearance. Did you think I was unaware of this? Would you tell someone they look good when they do not to feed their darkness and suggest they have to look that way? But telling someone you see their originality and effortful creativity shows gratitude and appreciation, which should always be welcome.

MY FIRST CONTACT

In August 2015, a client booked me for my first adventure in Sedona. Never did I feel more connected or at "home." It was the first time I had entered an advanced, highly vibrational, meditative state of being where I was wholly present and radiating love. Sedona awakened something in me that took me many years to recognize. My client was getting ready for dinner. I stepped outside, and immediately, I saw my first "UFO" hovering in the distance. I had this immediate connection to it. I felt like it either caught me or I caught it. It was not moving. I felt like it was there for me and was well aware of my presence. But because I was programmed to think something like that happening would be my "ego," it did not allow the connection I could have had, but something very special did happen. I was awarded something...maybe new insight. The craft was disc-shaped and seamless. This never made sense to me until later on; stay tuned. I yelled for my client and she caught it as it did, what appeared to be a loop, and it disappeared.

HEAL YOURSELF

"I do not wonder what happens when you spend more time charging than depleting do you?" - Master Nick Eagle

Our bodies are truly miraculous when it comes to their healing capabilities, and there is not enough appreciation for these abilities. It is a world full of people pretending that you are broken and that you need their product to heal.

Pharmaceuticals are the greatest scam and snake oil ever created. It has been proved many times over that they work as well as the placebo effect BECAUSE IT IS THE PLACEBO EFFECT. They do nothing but sedate, confuse, separate you from your soul and put a bandage over the problem. The placebo effect is taking a sugar pill (instead of the pill they are being told they are taking) in a blind (without the patient knowing) controlled study. And it has been determined many times that sugar pills have the same effect as pharmaceutical drugs. If you cannot add up what is happening, neither pill works, and people are "healing" themselves just because they are making the decision that they should no longer suffer. If you had ANY idea what we are.

How dare you ever even consider putting "food" inside of you that will make you a lesser being. And for what, mouth satisfaction? Have you ever sat with this thought? It is impossible to honestly think it is intelligent and benefits you more than not doing it. "Comforting eating" is one of the most foolish and destructive whispers from darkness.

The importance of what water you put inside yourself is greatly underestimated. MOST OF YOU are dehydrated and dying, even those of you who drink a lot of water. The best fountain of youth, the water of the Gods, is structured and filtered by nature. I highly recommend finding a place with a well or drinking filtered spring water without fluoride that does not come in plastic. And I do not dare even to wash my hands in unfiltered city water.

Tobacco is a very sacred plant that works well with other plant medicines and it can be cleansing, but it should never be inhaled. If you want to fight "God," this is a great way to do so, as well as inhaling the smoke from a campfire. You will pay.

At our creation and core, we are light. How dare the powers to ever suggest it is harmful to us if not abused? It charges, purifies and illuminates us like nothing else. It heals, makes us feel better and vibrate higher. It is source. It is "God." I recommend getting in the sun nude daily upon awakening and exposing all of you, including your genitals, as you build a protective layer, reset your circadian rhythm, charge and prepare for your day.

Going barefoot has an immediate and undeniable effect on our bodies on every level as we become saturated with electrons. This helps with enhanced cellular repair, neutralizing free radicals, reducing inflammation, and increasing energy and electrical activity in the brain, AKA, healing. Wearing rubber soles is one of the most foolish things we can do, especially when your toes are crammed into a shoe and natural movements are denied. Go barefoot, pay attention, increase your awareness and it will be something you will do often and not forget.

When we sleep, we heal. The most significant cause of disease and premature death is not getting enough sleep and not making our sleep productive. This world is filled with foolish zombies plugged into the matrix and running into each other. They never realize how deeply programmed they are by this world, which does not want them to connect to their higher self, make good decisions, or recognize that they do not need it and are better off without it. You must sleep alone. No partners or pets. If you think they do not disturb you, I encourage you to film it. As you decide to be happy and at peace next to them, you can also choose to be happier and more at peace being alone in a secure, cold, and dark area. Sleep should be a sacred act, and few people put enough thought into what happens during it. Most people are disturbed many times throughout the night, and just because you did not become fully aware of it or remember it, it does not mean that you did not suffer because of it.

Blackout the windows completely. Unplug all devices, including Wi-Fi and turn your phone to "Airplane Mode" so signals do not disturb your sleep and harm you. Put blackout stickers over all LED lights. I recommend not having any electronics in your room but if you decide to have a TV, cover it when not in use. Never sleep with mirrors in line with your bed; like TVs, they can serve as gateways and portals and disturb your energy.

Cleanliness is godliness. There should be no clutter in your house, but especially in your bedroom. Everything needs to have its place. You want to go to bed cold so your body can slow down and prepare. You want to be in a completely secure and locked-up area. Close off or cover your windows and doors with steel bars and keep your bed away from them. My new bedroom at home has no windows and steel doors. Never allow people to enter it or knock on your door without first scheduling an appointment with you. You do not even want the possibility of being disturbed in your mind. You never have to be up at a particular time or train yourself to never need an alarm. The thoughts of your phone ringing or an alarm waking you up can also greatly disturb your sleep, whether you realize it or not.

The direction of your sleep can also affect how well you sleep. North is the direction some civilizations believe the soul travels when it leaves the body, making it beneficial for astral projection or lucid dreaming. However, others suggest that it may cause blood and head problems due to the iron being drawn from the pull of the pole. Vastu Shastra, a teaching from India, advises sleeping with your head facing south or east. Experiment with different positions.

SINNING IS A THING

" I've yet to have one person tell me one sin that they must do."
- Master Nick Eagle

If you were born a sinner, you could just use that as an excuse for lacking guidance, effort and bringing us darkness. What a horrible trap that so many fall for, created by darkness. The truth is that you are distracted, not connected; you are not a teacher, and you will never tell me one sin that you must do.

If you knew better, you would not do it, period. People are not malicious; they know not what they do. There is "sin," but not how most view it. Sin is anything that fights "God." And with this sin, you will be stripped of power and connection, creating a lesser heaven. Suffering is a necessary warning letting you know you are making poor decisions. People suffer the most because they do not listen; they create fantasy worlds in which they pretend to know best and then they claim to be broken, have anxiety, depression and many other rewards from fighting "God." Either start taking better care of yourself, leaving behind fear, seeking truth, sitting in silence, listening and creating heaven or fight, run, hide, sedate yourself, and create hell.

DAILY AFFIRMATIONS

We do affirmations to remember our power and what we want to be, and when we are honest and own them, there is much peace and much power in doing so.

I post the most powerful affirmations on my X and in my Instagram and Facebook stories every day. Make sure you're watching them and turn on notifications so you see them all. Also, incorporate the Golden Laws of Enlightenment into what you need to work on. Everyone in my life, including followers, clients and students are asked to say one every morning and they are a part of my Enlightenment Protocol.

"I AM A LIGHT WARRIOR & I WILL NOT FEAR WAR"

"THERE ARE LAWS & I HAVE EVERYTHING I DESERVE"

"I WILL LEARN WHAT MY BEST SELF IS AND I WILL BE IT"

"THERE IS NO HARD THERE IS ONLY NECESSARY"

"TODAY I WILL BE ALWAYS NEVER BETTER"

"GOODBYE FEAR"

"PEOPLE'S WORDS WILL NOT AFFECT ME"

"I WILL CARRY THE WEIGHT OF THE WORLD ON MY SHOULDERS & I'LL STILL BE ABLE TO JUMP"

"I AM ONE WITH ALL & I AM A PART OF EVERYTHING"

"I AM NOT MY BODY I AM IMMORTAL & LIMITLESS"

"WHEN THEY FALL I WILL STAND TALL"

"EVERYWHERE I GO I WILL BE AN EXAMPLE TO ALL"

"I WILL NOT THINK THINGS I WILL KNOW THINGS"

"I WILL NEVER PUT LIMITATIONS UPON MYSELF"

"EVERYTHING WITHIN MY POWER, I WILL GRASP"

"I CALL BACK ALL OF MY ENERGY FROM ALL PEOPLE
AND ALL PLACES UNDESERVING"

"I WILL BE EVERYTHING THAT I'M SUPPOSED TO BE"

"I WILL TAKE IMMACULATE CARE OF ME & DISEASE
DOES NOT HAVE TO BE A PART OF ME"

"NOBODY WILL STEAL POWER FROM ME"

"I WILL BALANCE MY ENERGIES TO BRING THE
GREATEST FORCE TO THIS WORLD"

"I WILL CLIMB MOUNTAINS UNTIL THERE IS ALL BUT
PEACE"

"WHEN I CONNECT WITH MY SOUL THE UNIVERSE IS
ON MY SIDE"

"OTHER PEOPLE'S WORDS WILL NOT DESTROY MY INNER PEACE"

"I WILL NEVER BLAME EXTERNAL FORCES FOR MY PROBLEMS"

"I WILL NOT DO THINGS ONLY BECAUSE OTHERS DO THEM"

"WHEN I'M CONNECTED TO MY HIGHER SELF I CAN DO NO WRONG"

"I WILL NEVER APOLOGIZE FOR SPEAKING THE TRUTH"

"I BANISH EVERY TRACE OF ILL HEALTH WITHIN MY BODY BECAUSE I AM MADE IN "GOD'S IMAGE" AND I HAVE THE POWER TO DO SO"

"I AM A CHANNEL OF DIVINE HARMONY & HEALTH"

"I WILL INSPIRE THOSE AROUND ME BY MAINTAINING INSPIRATION WITHIN MYSELF"

"MY CELLS ARE FILLED WITH LOVE & LIGHT"

"EVERYDAY IS A NEW DAY & FRESH START"
"I WILL LEAVE BEHIND ALL THAT IS NOT SERVING
ME"

"I'M GOING TO LOVE ME...A LOT"

"I WILL FIND OUT WHAT I AM AND I WILL BE IT"

"I WILL NEVER TURN MY BACK ON FEAR, I WILL
ALWAYS FACE IT"

"THERE IS SUCH THING AS MAGIC & I WILL PROVE
IT"

"I WELCOME ALL EXPERIENCES LIFE HAS TO OFFER"

"WHEN I SPEAK MY WORDS WILL MEAN
EVERYTHING"

"I KNOW WHAT I MUST DO AND NOTHING WILL
STOP ME"

"I AM AS POWERFUL AS I DECIDE TO BE"

"WHEN THEY CHOOSE TO BE WEAK I WILL CHOOSE
TO BE EVEN MORE POWERFUL"

"I AM EVERYTHING I CHOOSE TO BE"

"I CHOOSE TRUTH & LIGHT"

"THROUGH TRUTH I WILL FIND ENLIGHTENMENT"

"I AM...EVERYTHING I SAY AFTER THESE WORDS"

"I WILL BE CONFIDENT SO I CAN CONNECT TO MY HIGHER SELF AND SERVE THIS WORLD SPIRITUALLY"

"I AM CONFIDENT BECAUSE I LEAVE BEHIND FEAR"

"I AM NOT HEALING I AM HEALED"

"I WILL BE MORE THAN A SMILE I WILL HARNESS GREAT POWER & LOVE"

"LOVE IS EASY"

"WHEN THE FEAR IS GONE ALL THAT'S LEFT IS ME"

"IT'S OKAY NOT TO KNOW"

"I AM ONLY INFLUENCED BY THE SPIRITS THAT I CHOOSE TO WORK WITH"

"MY CAPABILITIES AND POWER ARE LIMITLESS"

"I WILL NOT FEED DARKNESS BECAUSE I WILL
BECOME IT"

"I WILL LEARN WHAT I AM SO I CAN LEAVE FEAR AND
SUFFERING BEHIND"

"I WILL BE PROUD OF ME"

"I AM EVERYTHING I CHOOSE TO BE"

"I WILL BECOME PURE & LEAD THE WAY"

"I WILL BE A CONNECTION & GUIDE TO THOSE WHO
STRUGGLE TO REACH HIGHER REALMS"

"I WILL TRUST "GOD'S" DESIGN & THE LAWS I KNOW
WITHIN MY HEART"

"I WILL FLY LIKE AN EAGLE & LET MY SPIRIT CARRY
ME"

"I WILL RISE ABOVE & BE A PROTECTOR"

"I AM ALL POWERFUL & ALL CAPABLE"

"I WILL ONLY PUT THE BEST THINGS IN ME TO BE MY
BEST"

"I WILL STOP HIDING & LIVING IN FEAR & I WILL
STEP INTO THE LIGHT"

"I GET BACK WHAT I PUT IN"

"I WILL LIVE A LIFE WORTH SHARING"

"I WILL ALWAYS BE FULLY CONSCIOUS OF MY
BREATH"

"I AM RIGHT WHERE I'M SUPPOSED TO BE & I'M
LOVING EVERY MINUTE OF IT"

"I WILL BE HONEST ABOUT MYSELF & WHAT I TRULY
DESIRE I WILL ACHIEVE WITH EFFORT"

"I AM NOT A VICTIM I WILL NOT BLAME OR MAKE
EXCUSES"

"EVERY SECOND, I WILL BECOME MORE POWERFUL"

"THROUGH TRUTH I WILL FIND ENLIGHTENMENT"

"I WILL NOT DO THINGS ONLY BECAUSE OTHERS DO"

"EVERYTHING LIFE THROWS AT ME IS A CHALLENGE & OPPORTUNITY"

"I WILL INHALE THE POSITIVE & EXHALE THE NEGATIVE"

"I WILL GO INSIDE MYSELF TO FIND THE ANSWERS"

"TODAY IS GOING TO BE GOOD"

"I WILL PLAY ANY CHARACTER THAT I CHOOSE"

"I WILL BOND WITH NATURE & IN DOING SO I WILL BOND WITH "GOD"

"I AM EVERYTHING I NEED"

"I WILL SPEAK UP WHEN I KNOW MY VOICE WILL MAKE A DIFFERENCE"

"I WILL CHANGE MY VIBRATION TO MATCH WHAT I DESIRE"

"I WILL NEVER ALLOW DARKNESS TO CONVINCE ME THAT I AM BROKEN OR NOT CAPABLE"

"DARKNESS HAS NOTHING ON ME"

"I WELCOME ALL GUIDES, ANGELS AND EXTRATERRESTRIALS WHO SERVE THE LIGHT TO GUIDE ME"

"I WILL STAY IN TOUCH WITH MY SOUL & I WILL NEVER SELL IT"

"I WILL HEAL MYSELF & THEN I WILL HEAL OTHERS"

"I WILL BE GRATEFUL FOR EVERY BREATH"

"I WILL NOT SIT AROUND & WAIT FOR THINGS"

"I WILL BE MY MEDICINE"

"WITH EVERY BREATH I WILL BECOME MORE CONFIDENT"

"I COMMAND ALL BAD ENERGY TO LEAVE ME RIGHT NOW"

"I UNDERSTAND THAT WORDS ARE VIBRATIONS
THAT HEAL OR HARM"

"I WILL NEVER ALLOW EMOTIONS TO SEVER MY
CONNECTION"

"THERE IS NOWHERE TO RUN I AM RIGHT HERE"

"I AM A PART OF ALL THAT IS"

"I CHOOSE TO BE FILLED WITH LOVE & LIGHT & IN
DOING SO I GAIN MUCH POWER"

"NO MATTER MY PAST I WILL CHOOSE WHATEVER I
WANT TO BE"

"NOW IS ALL THAT MATTERS"

"I'VE GOT THE POWER"

"I WILL HAVE GRATITUDE FOR EVERYTHING THAT I
SEE"

"THE DARKNESS THAT I CARRY IS FROM MY CHOICES
& I WILL NO LONGER ALLOW IT TO BE A PART OF
ME"

"I WILL SWEEP AWAY THE CHATTER"

"I WILL NOT LISTEN TO THEM I WILL ONLY LISTEN DEEP INSIDE MYSELF"

"I AM ALL THAT I NEED"

"I WILL NOT BELIEVE ANYTHING. I WILL PUT IN THE EFFORT TO FIND THE TRUTH"

"I WILL STOP PRETENDING & I WILL AWAKEN"

"TODAY IS THE GREATEST DAY EVER"

"I CAN CHANGE THE WORLD AND I WILL"

"THE REAL "GOD" DOES NOT WANT ME TO FEAR IT"

"I WILL NOT SEEK MOTIVATION I WILL BE IT"

"I WILL LEARN WHAT I AM AT ALL COSTS"

"I WILL ALWAYS BRING PEOPLE UP & I WILL NEVER BRING THEM DOWN"

"I DO NOT GIVE UP"

"I AM GRATEFUL FOR THIS NEW DAY"

"I AM HERE TO IMPRESS I AM HERE TO INSPIRE"

"TO ALL THE PEOPLE WHO DOUBT ME
HA HA HA HA HA"

"I WILL TAKE ALL OF THIS WORLD IN"

"MY GRATITUDE WILL BE MORE THAN WORDS"

"I AM EVERYTHING I CHOOSE TO BE"

"I CHOOSE TRUTH & LIGHT"

"TROUGHT TRUTH I WILL FIND ENLIGHTENMENT"

"LOVE IS EASY"

"WHEN THE FEAR IS GONE ALL THAT'S LEFT IS ME"

"IT'S OKAY NOT TO KNOW"

"I AM ONLY INFLUENCED BY THE SPIRITS THAT I
CHOOSE TO WORK WITH"

"MY CAPABILITIES & POWER ARE LIMITLESS"

"WEAKNESS IS NOT ALLOWED IN MY BODY"

"I WILL LEARN WHAT I AM SO I WILL LEAVE
SUFFERING & FEAR BEHIND"

"I WILL BE PROUD OF ME"

"I LOVE TRUTH"

"I WILL PUT IN WORK & EFFORT & BECOME
CERTAIN"

"I WILL NOT JUST PRAY I WILL BECOME A PRAYER"

"I WILL NOT BE SCARED BECAUSE I KNOW HOW
MUCH IT HOLDS ME BACK"

"I WILL BECOME PURITY & DENY DARKNESS"

"I WILL NEVER BE STUCK BEING ANYTHING I DO
NOT WANT TO BE"

"I WILL FIND THE HEAVENS WITHIN & CREATE THE
HEAVENS OUTSIDE"

"I WILL HAVE MY LIFE ORGANIZED & I WILL BE PROPERLY PREPARED"

"I WILL NOT BELIEVE ANYTHING I WILL PUT IN THE EFFORT TO FIND THE TRUTH

"I WILL NOT WORRY I WILL INSTEAD TRUST"

"I WILL REMEMBER WHAT I AM"

"I WILL NOT CHASE WHAT I DESIRE I WILL BECOME DESERVING"

"I WILL NOT CREATE PROBLEMS I WILL SOLVE THEM"

"I WILL NOT ALLOW FEAR TO KEEP ME FROM BEING MY BEST SELF"

"I WILL NOT DO THINGS ONLY BECAUSE OTHERS DO"

"WHEN THEY CHOOSE TO BE WEAK I WILL CHOOSE TO BE EVEN MORE POWERFUL"

"I WILL BE ORGANIZED & PROPERLY PREPARED"

"I AM A HEALED WARRIOR"

"I AM NEVER ALONE WHEN I AM WITH MYSELF"

"MY POWER COMES FROM WITHIN"

"I AM WHAT I AM AND I AM EVERYTHING THAT I CHOOSE"

"TODAY I'M GOING TO BE INSPIRED"

"TODAY I'M GOING TO BE INSPIRATION"

"I WILL NOT ACCEPT MY FLAWS I WILL OVERCOME THEM"
"I WILL PROTECT MY ENERGY THROUGH TRUTH"

"I WILL NEVER RUN AWAY I WILL ALWAYS STAND UP FOR MYSELF"

"I WILL EMBRACE DIVINITY & I WILL BECOME IT"

AFFIRMATION NOTES

AFFIRMATION NOTES

SLOW DOWN

This is one of the first things I have people work on when they come to me. What are you in a hurry for? Life? It is happening right now. Did you not notice? Stop pretending that you are anywhere near your best when you are in a hurry. You cannot focus, be creative, connect, be patient, be loving......You are less respectful and you communicate poorly. You get NOWHERE. This "live fast and die hard" mentality is beyond foolish, as you destroy yourself, AKA, the world. You fool no one and nobody appreciates your energy, you tripping over your own feet and the scattered and chaotic thoughts that we all have to decipher.

Once we awaken and are connected, we flow and can complete things at extraordinary speeds without much energy, thought, tripping over our feet and making mistakes; however, if going at a fast speed is giving you anxiety, your teachers have failed you, as you live in distraction and fear. Those who choose fear must slow down and see the destruction.

BE DISCIPLINED

Self-discipline is the answer to all of your problems. It is about understanding your power and taking responsibility for your life. The definition is "the ability to control one's feelings and overcome one's weaknesses." It is an ABILITY. It is a choice. We should teach people they can be disciplined instead of being broken and incapable darkness conjurers.

You decide if you want to focus. You decide to be angry or happy and for how long. You decide how you feel and if someone saying or doing something will change that. You decide what you put in you knowing the consequences of doing so. If you cut your arm off, you can take responsibility for the foolish decision that lead to it, joke about not having to carry it around anymore and be grateful that you have a second, or you can be angry and pretend "God" hates you, blame the world instead of not understanding it and bring us more darkness.

You can do daily affirmations, yoga, meditations, read and write, be creative, spend time outside, exercise, prepare high vibrational and healthy meals and bring the world love and light, or you can not sleep, take drugs, chase money, exhaust yourself, watch movies and sports that only distract and you learn nothing from while consuming destructive and toxic food and substances, while pretending that you are incapable of evolving and you must bring the world darkness.

WE MUST CALL OUT DARKNESS

"Nothing is more enlightening than calling out darkness."
- Master Nick Eagle

The darkest people are those who pretend to have answers, usually to make money from others or attempt to steal energy and power from them by lying and claiming a higher status because they have nothing else to work with and no other way to keep their fantasy and fragile world held together.

They get their information from ignorant parents, other darkness feeders, social media influencers who found ways to get likes and follows by feeding and comforting darkness, corporations, celebrities, Hollywood and the darkest arts, modern Psychology. They attempt to prey on everyone they come in contact with. They pretend to be psychic empaths and teach astrology incorrectly. They often call people crazy and toxic. When you share exciting and positive news, they will respond with jealousy and envy, trying to turn it into something negative or something to be feared. They speak poorly of psychedelics because they never took them or took them before they were ready and chose fear over truth. Yet they support and take pharmaceuticals, alcohol, marijuana, Adderall and caffeine. You rarely see them off their phone or not playing loud music. They are unorganized, all over the place and trip over their feet. Their communication is abysmally poor, and they rarely speak or type a sentence that does not require deciphering or correction. Their pets and children are a representation of them and they are disobedient and suffer greatly from anxiety as well. They carry this boo-hoo, poor me, life is hard and mommy and daddy were mean to me darkness and energy around with them, as they blame the world outside of themselves and make endless excuses for their poor decisions and inadequacies. They do not seek truth; they put in little effort, live paycheck to paycheck, and demand free handouts while pretending to have a purpose through virtue signaling. They bring chaos and darkness to the world, and when you call them out on it, they throw around the words "judgment" and "projecting" to try to take the victim's stance. If you continue to press them, they will call you dismissive terms like "crazy," "psycho" or "narcissist" or blame your ego or past. They will do everything they can to avoid hearing your words or forget them immediately, and then pretend to bow out peacefully, while they are actually running away in fear. They say, "Let's agree to disagree," to try to escape it. They will try to say that your words are "your truth." They say that you "gaslight" as they do. Darker people will blame your zodiac. Even darker people will tell you that your demand for respect, focus, intensity, passion and caring is anger. They might even say, "Do you think you're a God or something?" They might say, "What do you think you're perfect?" They foolishly attack you because you have learned lessons that they decide to be too weak to hear. These are people who suggest "being human" means making mistakes. These people also think you should be "more humble," AKA, have a low estimate of your importance. The darkest ones will try to make you believe you have a sickness, parasites, or "demons" to try to get out of it. They never make any sense, but this talk usually confuses people and gets them out of it. Never bow to it. I recommend keeping a picture of these pages to show how unoriginal and predictable they are.

This is how I will begin my next book, "How To Battle Darkness." Stay tuned...

"YOUR TRUTH" IS LIES

"Never lie about what we are to make somebody comfortable."
— Master Nick Eagle

One of the evilest whispers of darkness tells you that you can call anything "your truth" and have it be truth. What happens to truth when you add a word to it? IT'S NO LONGER TRUTH. People are not bad or malicious and I see what they are "trying" to do, AKA, failing to do - reduce suffering by not "hurting feelings." However, they fail to calculate beyond the present. This is one of our most significant problems - virtue signaling. Too many people pretend they should be teaching when they fail to make great calculations. They fail to see the long-term suffering and destruction that allowing someone to lie in the present can bring, even if it brings them some brief peace.

IT IS ALL LESSONS

Stop trying to run away from your "problems" and escape your days that could have gone better. This is what those who suffer most do—one who lives Groundhog Day, day after day after day. Darkness loves those who are effortless and never learn anything. We must sit in stillness and silence with all our encounters and interactions, especially the ones that did not go as well as we would have liked. You must ask yourself, "What could I have done to prevent it from happening?" and, "What could I have done to have made it go better?" This is how we evolve and become better people. You bring nothing new to the world if you refuse to learn from all the lessons that present themselves, and you stay the same lost and confused person every day, who has very little to offer the world.

BECOME MORE AWARE

"Do you think that you could ever not get better at something?
- Master Nick Eagle

Do you have any idea what's going on inside you right now? What is the food inside you doing? Are you breathing through your nose or mouth? Are you taking deep breaths or disease-causing short ones? Are you aware that you are in control of your heart rate? How about emotions? Do you think we can get "songs stuck in our head?" What are your feet doing? What does your mouth and teeth taste like? Are you aware that you can sleep whenever you want and never need an alarm? Are you sitting or lying in a way that puts strain anywhere on your body, which will lead to bigger problems and suffering? Did you know that it is your body heat, not a blanket, that keeps you warm? Do you often fry your brain with artificial lights? Did you know that the sun is good for you? You don't wear the same shoes you wear in public in your house, do you? Do you have ANY idea what's on the bottom of them?

People pretend that they are "sensitive" because they decide to cry often. Real sensitive people, AKA, aware people, have an awareness of knowing the destruction of crying tears of poor me boo hoo and they do not do it. They also do not spend much time indoors, especially when exposed to artificial lights. They always have earplugs with them. They do not go anywhere near people drinking alcohol. They understand the world and only shed tears of understanding, ecstasy and joy because of its beauty, opportunities and possibilities. Do you have any idea what's out there and how not scary it is?

Focus on your breath until you are no longer breathing through your mouth. Wear a chin strap at night. Mouth breathing destroys you. It causes anxiety and disease. It can stretch and deform your face, nose, and jaw. When you breathe through your nose, you filter the air and properly control the temperature, moisture, and volume going into your lungs. Do this even when you train and hike. It strengthens your respiratory system and improves your lungs' ability to absorb oxygen. Do you have any idea what we become and how much peace and power one obtains when we become aware of things? What about when you become aware that it is you creating these destructive emotions? Now, what happens when you bring this awareness into your dreams?

GO "GOD MODE" IN YOUR DREAMS

Are you awake or are you dreaming?

Lucid dreaming is a form of next-level awareness mastery. You can develop the ability to build your dreams around you as you fall asleep and do whatever you choose. Picture yourself sitting cross-legged and shrinking. Do daily "reality checks" as you look around and ask yourself if you are awake or dreaming. I repeat the words, "I will know when I am dreaming, I will go God-mode and I will remember my dreams" most nights before bed. I also have tattoos that represent magical powers, lucid dreaming, astral projection, contacting deities, and God mode on my left hand, and I press the ones I desire as I drift off.

In my first lucid dream, I was staying at a client's house and I saw cows out the window. I wanted to ride an animal but didn't want to ride a cow, so I changed them into ostriches and went for a fun ride. I am now able to open portals and fly through space, visit people I know and go "God Mode." I can levitate and shoot lightning from my hands, and my psychic abilities are limitless. I can even contact deities and extraterrestrials. Most recently, I time-traveled.

HERE WE GO! MEETING THE KADOMA

In mid-2018, I was booked for four hours to be awakened. I have had endless people tell me that they see something in me. Most of you reading will agree. You see the fire in my eyes. You see a way out. You see truth and you see much love. Even if you don't push yourself, almost all of you push me to do better and rise above the darkness to do great things. I have been told angels follow me. Prophets and visionaries have said to me that I am chosen and here to do much good. I never paid much attention to it up to this point, but none have taken it to the level the "kadoma" did.

I was welcomed into the Las Vegas hotel suite by an older woman, who I could tell struggled with more than uncontained excitement and the fear of rejection. There was something bigger at stake. Before saying anything, she asked me to read sections of around 15 different books. All of them were stories told by prophets of people being brought to this planet to save it. Each story was unique and different. I struggled with my focus because I was unprepared for this. She asked me if any of them affected me. They did not.

She explained to me that God talked to her when she was younger and told her that she was responsible for finding chosen people and awakening them. She said it happened in a school classroom, and at first, she thought it was the PA system, but then she realized it was some other voice. She ignored it. I sensed it frightened her. Many years later, in her teens, she heard it again and attempted to talk back and ask questions. She determined it was "God." She said God did not reply, but angels did, although not in a clear manner. She was sent messages and images that were challenging to interpret. She told me that she had to tell me everything, and it was up to me to determine what it meant.

She then gave me all her old journals and asked me to read them. She insisted on bathing my feet with pure water from a glass picture and then rubbing dead sea salt, cocoa and oil on them as they did for Jesus before he walked the slums, she said.

She told me that the angels showed her all the world's suffering and directed her to study all religions, as they all contain truth. Her studies of religion took her to India. She first thought that she had to awaken the Dalai Lama. She often met with a man who lived and ate breakfast with the Dalai Lama. But this man told her that there was already a kadoma residing on the premises and the kadoma had already awakened the Dalai Lama. During the time of her trying to meet him, she stumbled upon Kama Sutra and sexual energy that eventually led her to me.

She said that upon seeing me on TV, she always knew I was one of the people she had to awaken. My book and practices confirmed it. She said I was the Maitreya Buddha. I had no idea what that was. She started losing me. She saw it. I disappointed her. She went on to tell me that I have the power to control time throughout the galaxy. She said I am here to revolt and liberate people through this sexual energy. She said I must unite us through song and dance.

She warned me to stay away from fire. I did not tell her, but I had a beautiful girl in my hot tub the prior weekend, whom I commented on liking the "fire in her eyes." I got the impression from her that she had done some unspeakable things from her stories. The kadoma, Karen, said to test her abilities, she picks horse winners but never bets because she will lose her powers if she does so. She said she picked a horse named "Bow and Arrow" and it won. This happened the same week, maybe to the day, I bought my first bow and arrow and touched one since my teens.

She told me that I needed to stop all the pedophilia in the world and relieve pressure on the Antarctic volcanoes that are overdue to erupt and will destroy the world if they do. She said it was because we were sucking all the oil out of the Earth. She said we were in the third simulation, and if we do not get this one right, there will be no more.

She was losing me more and more. I understood that "crazy" was not a thing at this point, but I saw her as incredibly lost and confused. I told her I would love to save the world, but I didn't know what to do with the information. She said to me, "I know it's you! You must wake up!!" I was watching her crumble in front of me. She was genuinely convinced that the many years of her life led up to this moment of my being awakened and soon after saving the world. I disappointed her more and more every second. I am in tears as I type this.

TAKE IMMACULATE CARE OF YOURSELF

"I wish you loved you as much as I love you."
- Master Nick Eagle

I go back and forth on the above quote. I know that many of my teachings and lessons aren't preparations for awakening, but rather to awaken now. And the above quote to one who doesn't seek truth would be turned off and run away. But it's true, I wish you and everyone else took care of themselves as well as I do. That's what it says. I've yet to meet someone who takes care of themselves better than I do. When I do, I will change the quote to, "I wish you loved you as much as "…" loves you."

We must learn what happens to everything we put inside of us. Not all food is equally created fuel. Why would one put anything but the cleanest and most efficient fuel inside of themselves? For the taste in one's mouth or an emotional attachment? How can have a weaker mentality? And most of the poison people eat doesn't even "taste" good. It's just filled with addictive and poisonous sugar and chemicals.

I am now one of the leaders in the world when it comes to the aging rate, and if you measure my telomeres, which is the most accurate way to measure your biological age, mine are more than 10 years behind my chronological age. Soon, I will prove that we can reverse age through my dietary and exercise practices, mixed with my yoga and meditation practices that most "bio-hackers" lack. I now call myself a "Spiritual Bio-Hacker." I do not take synthetic testosterone and my levels are best they can be. Most important is the brainwave state in which I operate and teach. I also use red light therapy, a hyperbaric chamber, and a sauna, and I do my own PRF injections. I have also created my "Enlightenment Protocol," which is my life's work and gift to you. It includes everything I eat, how to prepare it, supplements, exercise, yoga practices and more: nickeaglemystic.com/enlighten

THE KADOMA DID NOT GIVE UP

Messages continued to follow after our encounter:

August 18 2018 Hmmm in Justice League Batman calls out Wonder Woman for not getting out there. I am. And You've adjusted my trajectory to aim at volcanoes. That seems appropriate!! You're the Galaxy. I'll get to Ru, then You!

Aug 21 'the four d wave cern' google dat shiz 🌀

Aug 25 You are magical. Amazing things are happening. Vesuvius WILL get depressurized before she blows. You told me to focus on that and I have. You want to wake up - you will wake up. Thank you for coming to Earth 🌍🌎🌏🗻😎

Aug 26 Yer magical. Own it.

Sept 3 Happy Birthday! Thank you for coming to Earth

Sept 10 It's basically the exact same presentation, only Ru isn't a Scorpio, He's a Libra. Scales of justice, equality and balance. Ru and I have 20 years on you, that's why so much of what I said was puzzling. Perhaps Dr Strange had to wait on the porch for a similar reason. Best analogy ever: Donna and the 10th HAVE to 'do it' to unlock the Lionsgate...lmfao...ask a Dr Who fan.Smile more and wake tf up! Thank you for coming to Earth 🌍🌑🌍🏕️ 😎

Sept 11 Hmmm, facts: they have grooming schools for the pretty trafficked children, where they are taught to be sexy as children, but educated and taken care of, to be sold later. The ordinary looking ones are chained to beds and hit around 10 times a day. Wake up. Read yer emails Clark. Take the REAL challenge. Save the world!

Sept 12 2018 Omg, from your perspective, that was rather fast, but remember, it changed every morning for me.
1. I couldn't and still can't believe I ever found your show and the news led only to you. 2. You were an accessible person who could call Ru and Ru would pick up the phone. 3. Then I investigated you.

2. 4. Magical tattoo blessing kicked off stuff that is still incoming

including all those things I had to do and say - remember like the tape in 50 1st dates.

3. 5. So I apologize, if I had stuck to 'just a presentation to get you to pick up the phone, it would have gone way different.

4. 6. I always told the truth even if paint the car orange.

5. 7. Donna and the 10th 😎Thank you for coming to Earth.

Sept 12 2018 Consider the human shoulder, ain't no way anything like those statues exist with multiple functioning arms. Nope! It's motion. One of the things I went to India to check. I was right... well back then I was proving the Angels to myself. Anyway, you can't see the energy lines like in the movies, but you CAN make them. 😎

September 13 2018 Just in The Nick of time! 👍 🌍⛰️😎😎

Sept 14 2018 Page 59 of yer book. Can you see what I read? Anyway, Maitreya Buddha sits in a chair in readiness to quickly stand to help when needed. Hmmm? Up for the challenge or still lounging? Thank you for coming to Earth 🌍🌎🌏⛰️😎Your lounge chair! She's one of Your planets. Maybe clean Her up first...then lounge! ⛰️⛰️😎

Sept 15 2018 The Daleks and the Cybermen ain't NUTHIN compared to Yellowstone and Vesuvius. And Dr Who decided to take THIS lifetime off. What would Donna do? First she would

pay to see him....

Sept 15 2018 I'm trying to figure out if You're Amun. Ra is Ru, but they both got stronger together!

Sept 16 2018 So pretend you got an acting job to star as Lord Buddha, the Galaxy Incarnate, here to save Earth from a cold sore-like Virus that has run its course so now it's time for You to rewrite the DNA for this cell, Earth, who resides inside yer galactic Self! Thank you for coming to Earth! See, that was You! You said that in my head. 🧘🕶

In 2018, I went to Burning Man and experienced pains few ever will. I blew my back out on day one and spent a week screaming and crying in the back of my travel trailer, without being able to sit up, much less walk. A friend had to drive me back when it was over. Two weeks later, I was in for surgery. I guess I wasn't quite ready.

Sept 19 2018 Back surgery is a bad idea. There's a thin membrane of connective tissue that runs the length of the cord. It just needs to heal. Hope you got a 2nd opinion from a naturopath. Good luck and I'm right , Venerable Rinpoche Lord Maitreya Buddha. You did this to yourself! Unforced error.

Sept 20 2019 I pray for your speedy recovery. Really! Watch Dr Who. Start with Rose. I'm Donna, but The Nick Hawk should have made Donna FEEL LIKE ROSE, but you didn't. You showed up the 2nd day and let your gecko yell at me "there are no geckos". Get ready!! So, I feel like Donna, and Donna saves the Universe. Quit acting like Dr Strange BEFORE, and become one of the likable Timelords! Oh, and your planet's about to explode! ♪♫NEWS at 11♪♫

Sept 23 2018 Hmmm, if a Galaxy contacted one of His own stars and said 'this immune cell could only afford a small amount of my time, but perhaps if given enough time to explain herself, she might be found useful in curing the Virus that consumes Earth', then maybe I wouldn't have to rush. I will amuse Ru. My information is worthy of His time and Your time. Maybe keep dreaming you'll save the world, and you really will! Thank you for coming to Earth 🌍🦘🐰

Sept 24 2018 Wow. I'm right and you didn't help me. I did as I was told and you didn't simply get me to Ru. Whatever happens to humanity and Earth is on you. I'm a pawn, doing as I'm told! You should call Ru. Yer just being bored so why not save the world?! Thank you for coming to Earth 🌍🧗😎🦘🐰

Sept 26 2018 I'm a tool. I work for you, hence what happened. If I'm right, everyone else is wrong, including Nick - not Maitreya - Nick. I appreciate the fact that you hate being wrong but you are. Of course there are r complex geckos running home to the

TV every single night. And there are Very Special people called Incarnates or Venerable Rinpoches. Dude, wake up before you hurt yourself again, or worse, before you ruin your own plan through inaction. You really think you came to hell to surf? Really? Watch Dr Who and wake up Timelord.

Sept 27 2018 I suppose it's possible that you're not anything special and that was all just a coincidence....... 😄😄😄😄😄😄 😄😄😄😄😄😄😄⊠. Thank you for coming to Earth 😄😄😄 😄😄😄😄😄😄I so love you like a brother - one who happens to be a Time MF Lord. Wake the fu*k up, Nick A coincidence 😄 😄😄😄😄 ⊠ Calculate those odds 😕😄😄🐰😄😄😄Pokémon for Maitreya Timelord SupermanPain is real. Mine and yours are irrelevant compared to those kids. We can save them. Understand that gangsta rap is 'evolved gecko' rap or 'angry cornered dragon' rap. If we turn them to empowered, enlightened dragons, and show them they were being used and groomed to be stupid entertainment war tools for the Virus, well then, there's an Army. Ru is also black. I get sick. Don't let me die. Please help me I'm starting to give up on you

MY CRUCIFIXION?

As I look back, none of it was "hard." Nothing is ever "hard." It is a deplorable decision to decide that something necessary for you to be what you are supposed to be is "hard." I suffered through the most pain one can endure in the week of my second Burning Man. I blew my back out on day one and spent a week screaming and crying in my trailer, not being able to sit up, much less stand-up. I got a ride back and went straight to the ER. I had to take pain pills to get up every day and sleep. I had nerve pain going down through my legs and testicles. It felt like I got kicked in them 24/7.

Three weeks later, I had my back fused. It was the worst herniation the doctor had ever seen, and I was the first patient he had not to touch pain pills after. I had the good news that jiu-jitsu was a go after I healed, because my spine was in such good health. The doctor couldn't believe my arm pain had gone away. He thought for sure I had another blown disc in my neck, and he said there was no way my back injury could cause the arm pains. He was wrong.

I went five days, and I thought I was coming around, but I went back to popping pills three times a day to function. It was not healing for some reason. I was now three weeks deep into pills and lost. I took one last trip to the doctor's office, 40 pounds lighter, as I pushed a walker into his office, crying. The X-ray showed everything was okay. He did not have one recommendation to improve my life.

I could barely think. I could not even figure out the best way to kill myself. I could not live another day like that. It was a good run. Tomorrow, I might be shooting myself if I can find my gun. That night, I gave myself one more mental push and meditated deeply.

It was the bed! The next day, I barely made it into a mattress store. The salesman had to help me on the beds as I cried. I decided to get an adjustable bed and a firm mattress. They delivered it the next day. The day after that, I woke up and immediately knew I would now heal. A few weeks later, I could start training lightly. Over-training would often lead to nerve pain activation, following me falling on the floor and more screaming and crying, usually for 40 minutes at a time, as I looked down from above and wondered why I was crying. It was just pain, and I have already felt it all. Oh yeah, my tailbone also curved into my anus, and it felt like I had a sick up it 24/7. A year later, I overcame, rose again and was ready for anything and more with this new start and appreciation. It was time to learn what I really was. No more distraction. No more fear.

NEVER HAVE A BAD DAY: BE ALWAYS NEVER BETTER

When someone asks me how I am, I sometimes reply, "What a silly question; why would we ever choose to be anything but amazing?" But my favorite reply is, "Always never better." I have not had a bad day since I received my Brazilian jiu-jitsu black belt on the podium after winning a tournament. There are a few accomplishments that require more work. It takes more hours than it does to become a medical doctor. That day, I gave myself one of the greatest gifts one could ever give. It far surpassed winning a jiu-jitsu tournament and receiving a black belt. If you're doing the things you're supposed to be doing and have the mindset you're supposed to have, you will never have a bad day. Don't you dare sit there and pretend you must. "God" doesn't want you to have bad days and you shouldn't.

THERE IS NO "TRY"

"You either do or try to do." - Master Nick Eagle

You either do something or try to do it. Trying is not doing. Instead of being on a path, be at the destination. Instead of "healing," be healed. It is all decisions. Everything is a choice. All this "trauma" is your creation. You can just as easily decide to accept something and become a stronger and wiser person, as you can decide you are hurt, broken, and weak because something happened. Do not try to understand who you are; figure it out. Your excuses and lies are effortless and weak. People who don't make them can see through them and even come up with better ones. It's amazing how those who try most things never try to lack effort.

MY FIRST FULL CHAKRA KUNDALINI AWAKENING

In August 2019, I returned to Burning Man, hoping to make up for the prior year. I was healed, prepared, and becoming increasingly pure. I asked for more answers.

After consuming some psychedelic mushrooms, I was riding a bike along the Playa when we stumbled upon a structure I would not usually be so drawn to. There were endless ones. Some shot fire, and some you could play on. But there was no choice. I immediately proceeded towards the middle of it. It was not the beauty of the structure that drew me, but the energy.

I sat down and took a couple of breaths. It was no longer the "me" that I knew at the wheel. I was one with a greater force and began to be guided by it. I sat cross-legged for the first time in my life for a few seconds. I started taking bigger and deeper breaths. I soon began doing holotropic breathwork, which I had not even known was a thing. I was doing pelvic floor and abdominal squeezes while I pushed my tongue to the roof of my mouth and rolled my eyes toward my third eye. I began shaking violently as if I were having a seizure. I was practicing ancient kriyas that I had never been taught. I didn't know what a kriya was, either. If it weren't for my hands being in a prayer position in front of me for the first time in my life, my energy and the spinning Merkabah light vessel around me, people might have thought I was in trouble. No, I did not know what a Merkabah light vessel was either. After a few minutes? I came to. My friend said, "I think you just had a kundalini awakening." I replied, "What's that?" I mastered yoga and meditation without instruction from another man. This was one of our greatest feats of our existence and I had NO IDEA what was happening. This should go down as one of our species most historical moments.

Throughout the night, I continued having these experiences. Never had I felt such love, understanding and power. It helped me solve so many riddles in my head. My friend kept checking in to see if I was okay because they were intense. And I kept replying, "I am perfect, how are you?" The fifth time, he began to cry. He told me he felt like I was sucking the energy from him. I stood up and hugged him. I felt and connected with every cell in his body. I helped induce his first awakening. It was beyond beautiful. I have now acquired what most would consider an unimaginable power. I did my first major healing through touching someone.

Two days later, I went back to the structure without being on any substances, and I was able to induce another kundalini meditation; it was just nowhere near as intense. I can induce them without psychedelics, but it is nothing like with them. The right shaman, music, gong and energy all play a role. In my last Las Vegas booking, I had one in the bathroom of a casino because I posted something beautiful, and all of the loving feedback from my followers took me there. I have them driving into Sedona, and I also have them on my land, behind my home, when I hike to Nick Eagle Peak, among many other areas around Sedona, when I watch superhero movies, and when I walk into the produce section in Whole Foods.

I want to report that the structure in which I had this awakening is called "The Chapel of the Chimes." I hope to rebuild it at Eagle Vortex Awakening Sanctuary someday. I am in talks with the creator, who was very happy to hear my story. It is costly and large, and I would have to build a structure around it to protect it. I am also currently maxed out on my budget. But I will be accepting donations to help make it and you will have a plaque with your name on it inside if you do.

HAVE AN INFLATED SENSE OF SELF-IMPORTANCE

The darkest, most overused, and least understood word in our language right now is "narcissist." I hate even typing it. How dare one suggest you can exaggerate your sense of importance? There is a place for all of those who use dismissive words and they live it every second. They lack a profound understanding of what we are. You should have an excessive interest and admiration for yourself; it should be higher than what it is right now and higher than the average person on this planet at this time.

You probably do not understand what you are and what you are capable of. Most of you pretend to be something else, but you know. Deep down, you know. You feel it. It wants to come out. You just fear what will happen when you go with it and go within. Most of the world will turn on you and try to bring you back down to their level. You must be strong. You must rise out of the pits in which they scheme.

333

While sleeping in the sacred healing dome at Eagle Vortex, I had numbers sent to me twice one night. Both times, "333." I woke up the second time and didn't think much of it. I failed to remember what those numbers meant. I was never a numerology person and didn't pay much attention. No, I did not think seeing 11:11 meant angels were sending you messages. So I went back to bed. The next day, I had forgotten until later that evening. I decided to look up what "333" meant and the first thing I read said something similar to:

"The essence of the holy trinity. The mind, body and spirit are present with 333. The universe is letting you know that you are being watched over by Ascended Masters and you are safe and secure. Jesus is the Ascended Master who is linked to 333 and best known for it. Buddha, St. Germain, Moses and Quan Yin are linked as well. The message is to remind you of the courage and strength you hold and to keep moving forward with your spiritual growth."

Yes, I was blown away again. Soon after that, I realized my phone number contained 333. Soon after that, I realized my birthday is 3x3, 3, 3x3x3. I always knew it was a special combination of numbers, but it didn't hit me until after the dream. I no longer believe in coincidences and even the biggest skeptic would find this minimally interesting.

BE AN OPEN BOOK

"Do not judge a book by the cover but judge it after you read it."
- Master Nick Eagle

There should not be one thing in your life that you fear or feel guilty about. It is all lessons. By being open, you teach others that we should never look down upon someone because of their lack of guidance or experiences unless they are dishonest about it. When you create guilt from something that you once did and fear what people may think of you upon finding out, your messages and teachings are lies. They do not help anyone and they do not allow people to help you properly. There are valuable lessons to be learned from doing so. They show that you have overcome. I once had panic attacks and horrible stage fright, and now, I couldn't be more confident. This tells you that we are all capable of overcoming and lying about it will never allow you to.

MY SECOND TIME HELPING SOMEONE INDUCE A KUNDALINI AWAKENING

Over the next couple of years, I would eat mushrooms and attend ayahuasca ceremonies every so many months. These divine and sacred substances allow me to induce these meditations with ease. I never force them. I only have them when they call, but the bigger the dose, the more they call.

I had a very powerful ceremony with a friend who was greatly struggling. He was expecting a child in the next couple of weeks, and his ex-girlfriend did not want him in the room. His business was not doing as well, and he struggled with a marijuana "addiction," AKA, running from his fears.

\After a powerful 30-minute Awakening Session, during

which I helped him realize that his energy is what is failing this world and that he needs to take more responsibility for his life, I began having one of my "God-mode" meditations in front of him. I sometimes enter "God-mode" when I awaken people, and my powerful words of encouragement tend to induce this state in me. After a couple of minutes into mine, I noticed he began to breathe as if he were hyperventilating. When I take my breaths, I breathe differently than he did, so I thought something was wrong at first. But then I got up and saw what was happening. I smiled from ear to ear.

It was much different than my first time. I was able to embrace it. I once said, "I did not peek in the door; I ran through it." He was stuck. He was fighting. I sensed too much fear. I gave him words of encouragement, such as, "You are being born again," and I performed my first energy cleansing, also known as Reiki work, on another human with my hands.

It passed and he entered a blissful state. I no longer recognized my friend sitting across from me on the couch. He was glowing. He told me he physically felt something leave him. I am unsure if he confused this for the Kundalini energy release, but he was reborn. Over the next couple of weeks, he could not thank me enough. He told me he would have given me everything he had to experience that night, and he ended up watching his child being born and his business boomed.

STOP BEING "NICE"

I wrote a book on this. Who do you think of when you think of "nice" people? I think of salespeople and politicians. I do not picture respectable people whom I look to for answers. I do not think of people that I want to spend my time with. I see people making small talk and giving weak compliments to sell them something or take advantage of them. The nicer people are, the faker and darker they are. I see disingenuous and lost humans trying to trick me because they fail to figure anything out. I see people who are afraid to challenge anything or anyone. I see people who poison themselves and pretend everything is all good. I see people who do not focus. I see people who trip over their own feet. And I see most of you enabling them and pretending right along with them that they make good decisions and put effort and energy into serving the world. Fake smiles should be frowned upon. We must teach them that their fantasy world is nonsense and lies, and they do not deserve attention or admiration simply for being nice. Do not confuse genuine kindness, caring, and respect with nice.

CALCULATE EVERYTHING

Stop doing things just because you've always done them. Stop doing things because it's all you've seen. Stop doing things because it is all you know. Stop doing things without intention and purpose. Do not even do things with just purpose; do things with the highest purpose. I know it takes work and effort. Calculate that work and effort pay off already.

SO WHAT HAPPENED DURING MY KUNDALINI AWAKENING?

Googling "Kundalini Awakening" took me to Buddhism. Years later, I discovered that everything I had done, including the shaking, was an ancient technique to induce these states and awakenings by activating the brain—the postures direct energy. The squeezes send fluid up the spine. When they happen, I connect to "God" and enter advanced states of Samadhi. Here, I obtain answers, heal, astral travel, acquire great power and more.

I was pleasantly surprised to discover that Buddhist teachings align with many of my own. It started making more sense why this happened to me and why I was able to do things that Buddhist masters and lamas spent a lifetime hoping to achieve. I've searched everywhere to find someone who has done what I have done and failed. I have found some people who have experienced kundalini awakenings, many more who say they have, but not one who has had a full chakra awakening. And believe me, I would know. Yes, plenty have tried to convince me.

Just before my Costa Rica ayahuasca ceremony, around March 2021, I shared the story of the kadoma with a friend. When I was sharing it, I Googled "Maitreya Buddha" for the first time since hearing the name many years back. I read something about the "Maitreya Buddha" coming here and awakening the world through "Kundalini energy…"

…Your hair should be standing up right now...

...Something hit me. I did not remember reading that in my prior search. If I did, it probably didn't stick because I didn't know what that was. My world started changing. How could that be a coincidence?! What is going on???

NEVER BE BORED

Develop a greater appreciation for stillness and silence. Have more appreciation for what happens when you do. Develop a deeper appreciation for healing through the breath. Have more appreciation for life by properly digesting it and taking it in. How dare one ever be bored? How do you not have a list of a thousand things you want to accomplish and see and see again? But you need to see everything properly. I started traveling too much. I stopped appreciating it as much. I felt like I was seeing the same thing. Give yourself time to heal, digest and take the world in properly. Spend this time figuring out the best way to accomplish everything you want to achieve and see.

NEVER BE TIRED

The greatest secret to living a long, Godly life is never to push yourself past the point of destruction. We live in a world where people often try to convince you to work out, even when it doesn't call, and wake up early and work 18 hours a day to be rich. This is hell. Most people are unaware that they are part of it. Imagine how much longer everyone would live if they had one or two extra productive sleep cycles a night. Would they die? If we heal when we sleep, can we overheal? How about age backward? Most of you, the first time you become fully conscious in the morning, convince yourselves it is time to start working. If you knew the benefits the first time you became fully conscious after a sleep cycle, you would tell yourself you have one or two to go. Stop pushing through everything. When you are yawning, you are dying. Hope to one day be conscious after every sleep cycle and know when your body is done healing.

BE COORDINATED

I have had numerous people and clients attempt to convince me that they were born uncoordinated; one even claimed to have the "uncoordinated gene." How could one understand themselves any less? Does this mean you cannot become more coordinated, or is there a limit to how coordinated you can be? You are suggesting that I was born coordinated. How dare you discredit my effort. No baby exits the womb doing cartwheels and walking tight wires. Nobody does cartwheels and walks tight wires without much guidance and training. People are uncoordinated because nobody taught them they could be. They never had any inspiration or motivation to put the work in to become it. It's not their fault, but stop feeding their darkness and allowing them to pretend they have to trip over their own feet and suffer.

DID ANGELS OR EXTRATERRESTRIALS PREPARE ME?

Before my greatest awakening in Costa Rica, I had "visits." During all of them, I felt the most loving presence. One put me to tears of ecstasy as I was painting and cooking lamb chops. I had given up meat many times and failed while losing massive amounts of weight, turning white and looking dead. Once, I managed to make it six months, but I was in terrible shape, so I went back to eating it. But the night I was cooking the lamb, I had a visit and I ended up feeding the lamb to my dogs. I continued to eat meat, but this suggests that something special was happening with me. Were they guiding me? Preparing me? Pushing me? Was it me? I have now been meat-free for years, and I will not be going back. Discover how I maintain my size and vigor with the Enlightenment Protocol.

ANYBODY CAN BE ANYBODY'S SOULMATE

Anybody can "fall in love" with anybody else. I never recommend falling while doing anything but having much gratitude and appreciation for someone who puts in much work and that you greatly admire is a beautiful thing. To have everyone "fall in love" with you, all you have to do is be greatly connected to our soul. We are "falling in love" with ourselves at our best. All you have to do is take immaculate care of yourself, leave behind fear and put truth above all. Why don't you? Why do you refuse to be honest about why you don't? Why do you seek and attempt to take light from those who have? Why don't people admire you like they do the innocence and light in children? You choose fear. You choose darkness. You do not have to. You can be wise. Sit in silence. Get to know yourself. If you don't like being around yourself, why would you ever think someone else would? Do you just want to find someone else to drag you down with you? How dare you ask for a soulful presence when you refuse to connect to yours?

MEDITATE

I am surprised at how often I am asked about meditation. If it were taught in school or church, we would be enlightened in one generation. Most people consider it an advanced and challenging practice. All you have to do is sit in a lotus position or lie down, close your eyes, and remain still. It works like magic. It is magic.

As I have already communicated, the goal is to connect to your higher self, AKA "God" or source, to obtain this ancient wisdom and enter states of healing. Now, this should be easy, but most of you are so poorly programmed that you can't even close your eyes for a few seconds without crying, much less quiet your mind to heal and obtain wisdom.

If you refuse to quiet your mind to connect because of distractions, you need to put energy into eliminating them. Now, what do you do to carry all this panic and anxiety? Is it because you make good decisions or could you maybe make better ones?

I recommend storing all questions, thoughts and to-dos in a calendar and note application on your phone or in a notebook. I recommend avoiding all stimulates. The goal is peace; they do not bring you peace when you're on them or withdrawing from them.

You must also learn how to be done with "work" and chasing money. If you knew just how much more money would come your way if you spent more time caring for yourself and meditating.

You need charging and energy to meditate and connect. Don't exhaust yourself all day and think you can benefit from meditating while being exhausted. Nothing special will happen. Stop doing everything when you are exhausted. Nothing good comes out of you, your brain doesn't work, you're not creative and you do not solve problems. GO TO BED.

You can focus on breathing and chants but do not use them as a crutch to quiet the mind. All you have to do is realize what you are and stop pretending you cannot simply not think of stuff. "Aum" is a mighty chant that represents creation and love. The goal is to create a "God frequency," have it ring throughout existence and call the attention of many beautiful beings.

Yes, the end goal of meditation is awakenings and enlightenment, and yes, this should be the goal. Do not turn the page, forget this and continue your life of nonsense, chaos and distraction.

Go to nickeaglemystic.com and click "KUNDALINI" for more info and videos.

MASTER NICK EAGLE "GOD-MODE" MEDITATION

Almost everything that I now do comes from being connected to and listening directly to "God." I know of no other who has been "shown" yoga, meditation and reiki through meditation. I hope to find others. My yoga movements, kriyas, meditation and breathwork all come directly from "source." And when you go directly to the source, this is where you find truth, the real answers and much peace and power. I no longer do things because others do. I no longer teach things because someone once taught me it. I no longer pass along my teachings without knowing they are the greatest methods to take you to "God" and have the best chance of leaving behind pain and suffering. If you wish to learn how to meditate properly, you are at the right place.

What I'm about to share with you are the most advanced yoga practices and meditation techniques. They might not be the best place to start, but that is your choice, and the simple choice of deciding whether you are ready to listen or not will determine that. So this potentially could be how to meditate for beginners and beginners should at least have this understanding of the goal when they begin.

We should only do things when our body calls for it, but to do so, you must be a masterful listener. You must know what your body calls for. Too many of us are programmed not to do things because others convince us that they're hard or we can't, and they harm us instead of heal us. Those who do not work out and exercise often do not do so because they have a limited understanding of their body and its benefits. They are the worst listeners because if one listened to their body, they would know that the body wants to move often and be stretched and taken care of and built. The main reason we weight-train is to improve bone density and strengthen everything from our tendons and ligaments to our joints, not just our muscles.

For a long time, I have recommended that you do a hard full-body workout every other day, and if you miss a day, you do the next no matter what, forever, and I still stand by this. But the movements you are doing and the intensity of these movements must come from listening to your body. I no longer have a predetermined workout session that I follow, except for rotating back and chest muscles as my main lifts.

I no longer decide the weight I'm using beforehand and do not count the reps or sets. My body tells me what to do and what it wants. I no longer foolishly lift hefty amounts of weight for only a few repetitions. I typically do ten to thirty repetitions and three to six sets of everything that I do, but this will vary every workout. See my "Enlightenment Protocol" for more information.

Now, this is important to understand because we will be applying the same principles to our meditation techniques, yoga and breathwork. I do not want you to attempt to release kundalini energy and delve deeply to heal and find answers when you are not operating at high levels and are in a heightened state, because it will not happen and could deplete you if you attempt it when not ready. You must be worthy and deserving. You must take immaculate care of yourself. You must put truth above all and you must leave fear behind. If you do not do these things, you will not be able to enter these advanced states. So few ever do; many lie and pretend they do. You must be godly. You must follow all of The Golden Laws of Enlightenment.

Now, for those who operate at high levels and are truly ready to release kundalini energy, I will walk you through what happened to me when I entered a state worthy of being shown these practices by "God." You must be in a constant state of meditation, be at complete peace and have nothing but gratitude and appreciation for this gift of life. When I enter these states, I make contact with extraterrestrials and I have kundalini awakenings. Thinking and writing about it right now is beginning to induce one. And when you operate at high levels and you listen it will call. To achieve these states, I highly recommend following my free "Enlightenment Protocol," which includes taking immaculate care of yourself, practicing morning affirmations, and more, including advanced healing techniques.

When it calls, you must go to a place of complete peace, away from all disturbances. If you have practiced the "lotus position" and are comfortable there for an extended period, I highly recommend doing that. If not, you may lie down. Start by taking deep breaths through your nose, completely filling your diaphragm. As this breath fills you, so will "God." "God" is the breath within the breath. Bring your hands in front of you in "prayer position." Many teach to touch them to your heart chakra and there are benefits, but I was shown to keep them out in front of me as far out as possible while keeping a 90° bend in the elbow and your hands together. Keep breathing deep and hard, and as deep as it calls, and as hard as it calls. When it calls, it can be called to be very intense as you suck in as much air as you can through the nose as fast as possible, completely filling yourself with air and releasing it through the mouth as quickly as possible. If it calls, press your tongue to the roof of the mouth and bring the eyes towards the middle of the forehead up towards the third eye. After so many breaths, which can vary from a few to multiple minutes worth, you'll get to a place where you should take one deep breath, hold and squeeze your sphincter and pelvic floor muscles tightly (I recommend doing 200 pelvic floor squeezes every 2-3 days to strengthen and help this process). If you're operating at high levels and listening correctly, you are now one with the gods, and you have entered a state of peace, healing, and answers.

When it calls and I begin the breaths, I shake quite violently; the blind eye would think that I am having a seizure. I used to think that I was generating energy while doing this and that it was a consequence of the actions, but after reading about this and sitting in meditation with the thought of these actions, I determined that it is also an ancient meditation technique to induce advanced states. I also practice other mudras when they call. The Dharma Chakra Mudra is very powerful.

You must learn how to meditate properly if you seek to operate at the highest levels and enter advanced states. Most do not desire what I do because they have no idea what is possible. I've become worthy of sitting with the gods and I know that anyone on this planet can join us. I am awakened, an awakener and you should listen to me.

111

MY GREATEST AWAKENING: THE COSTA RICA CEREMONY

In Costa Rica, I was not expecting anything too spectacular to happen. The thought of being the Maitreya Buddha awakening the Earth with kundalini energy was not even a thought I was exploring.

The retreat center was situated beside a river that flowed through it. It had fun housing and sleeping huts spread out, horses, a wall-free community dining center, and a huge wooden yoga studio/ceremony area sitting high up in the canopy, where you could open the large windows and be one with the giant trees, creatures, and jungle. It inspired me a lot with Eagle Vortex. I would love to return.

This was the typical weeklong ceremony, where you drink ayahuasca three times throughout the week, never on back-to-back days. Lots of ceremonies are just over the weekend and you drink medicine three nights in a row. I consider this to be destructive, foolish, and abusive if you drink a lot every night, as many do, and as most "shaman" allow, as they collect their money. I once didn't know this, and I used to drink two large servings every night. You need time to process and recover between nights. Ayahuasca is the most sacred and special medicine and there are consequences when you abuse it. And when you drink it a lot, the effects also diminish, and it can be damaging. I have a friend who helps orchestrate ceremonies, and she does not feel the effects anymore, and it is not all she does not feel.

NOCHE UNO

On the first night, I now always drink only a small cup and hold down the fort. It is a heated blend of the ayahuasca vine and chacruna leaves, which makes a thick soup. I am the only person I have ever heard of who enjoys the brew's taste. The ceremony begins in silence as the sun goes down, with everyone sitting in stillness, followed by whistling and protection songs.

I can tell you with great accuracy who in the group will purge or should purge before the night begins. I have drank ayahuasca over 30 times, and I have never purged. I would not dare disrespect the medicine like that. And the purges from most are usually purges of darkness, lies and fear that I do not hold. Purging only tells you that you have more work to do, you might not have been properly prepared and you might not have been ready. Purging can be beneficial and bad "spirits" can leave you, but most of the time, you do not significantly benefit from the purge, even if you feel better afterward. You only feel better because you are no longer being judged by "God" and can, once again, run away. Purging can be a distraction and prevent you from connecting to obtain the healing benefits. The ones purging and crying and trying to sleep it off shouldn't even be there. They were not properly prepared, ready or deserving. Having a purge and returning to a place of gratitude and appreciation is another thing. Unfortunately, most "shamans" only comfort those having these nights and never tell them the truth of why they have them. The truth is, you can either choose fear, decide to feel bad, lie about what you are and vomit in your bucket or choose truth, accept and understand, take responsibility for the darkness you bring and sing and dance. All true shaman will get you up and dancing.

I look after those who lack experience. I've yet to see a "shaman" properly prepare someone. I connect with everyone in the room. I send love and light to all, while providing comfort and support. I can now guide people out of the darkness from across the room. I make sure to hang out in the public areas after the ceremony and the next day to speak with anyone who needs someone to talk to. I bring people peace and calm everyone down so I can blast off the second night...

NOCHE DOS

It was my turn. I started with a large. I had the opportunity to witness the most musically talented and beautiful "shaman." Although he failed to prepare guests properly, he is a very lovely being. It always takes the right combination of energy and song to induce my meditations, and they usually don't happen until I take the second cup and have the right song, usually a cleansing one. Tonight was different. From the first note of the first song, I was gone. I don't even remember what song it was. I should not say gone because I was everywhere. But I was no longer just in the studio. The breathing and shaking I do can be quite distracting and I usually inform my neighbors and try to contain it as much as possible, but not this night.

You would be filled with curiosity and appreciation if you had any idea of what was happening. You would allow the loving energy that pours through me to charge you, and if you paid close enough attention, I would take you with me.

Behold my first major spirit animal encounter. Can you guess which one visited? I chose the name Nick Hawk 10 years prior when I was in the entertainment business, and decided to have a stage name. It was the first that came to me on the first attempt of a thought and I just went with it. I had zero attachment to hawks at the time, that I was aware of. I later came to appreciate everything they represent: protection, connection to higher realms, and spiritual awareness.

It was a bird. The first vision was the head in a kaleidoscope pattern and it seemed to be a hawk. I felt it charging and connecting with me. The second vision was a huge hawk-like bird hovering in front of me and flapping its wings. It charged and connected even more. I never felt so much power. In the third vision, it landed on my knee and wrapped its wing around me and protected me as it looked around.

I told someone about the encounter and described the bird as a "dragon hawk." The next day, I was reading a book on shamanism and read that spirit animals come to you in threes. There was also a picture of what visited me, and it was an "eagle-hawk." No, I promise I have not seen this before. Yes, I was mind-blown again.

Weeks later, a client ordered an Awakening Session from my website to discuss the encounter because I posted about it on social media. She told me she spent much time studying spirit animals, and "it is like one in a gazillion" and "practically unheard of in shamanic circles" for one to hug you. Upon further research, I discovered that what she said was indeed true. But if this loses you, you won't make it through night three. It is all going in here and I have to tell you everything. This was just the beginning of night two...

NOCHE DOS PARTE DOS

My "God Mode" meditation continued. The eagle-hawk filled me with so much power. The next thing I know, I am being blasted with light from source in space. When I say blasted, I mean being struck with great force. It was "God." As I absorbed this thick, golden light, my aura thickened with it, perhaps five inches of dense light radiating even more. I became one with the "Gods." I was anointed. With this light came visions, not only of healing myself, but also of healing others with my words and by placing my hand on their foreheads. I later realized I was being shown true Reiki healing but without the symbols.

Then came visions of turning my Vegas home into a public place of worship. To worship us. To have great appreciation for what I have become, the opportunity for all of us to become this and to express gratitude for this gift of life. To awaken others. To teach. To have beautiful prayers for creation and opportunities, instead of begging a false "God" in the sky that you are taught to fear and who will give you things because you beg him. I figured out how to leave behind fear and no longer suffer. I now needed a place for people to come to seek my guidance and wisdom. I was now trusted by "God" to pass along its message and I was given the keys to the castle.

MASTER NICK EAGLE PHD

NOCHE TRES

On the third night, I was unsure if anyone living had ever undergone the change I had. I was on a path for many years, but I finally arrived. It all made sense. I became all-knowing and all-powerful. When most, maybe all, speak the word "enlightened," they have no idea of what they say. I considered not sharing this information due to the potential repercussions and backlash, but I have decided to share it with everyone who is ready to hear it, even if some who hear it are not ready, because then they would have to admit why they are not.

I was charged, but I was still a little exhausted from the previous night. Ayahuasca helps you connect to amazing places but also depletes you in ways. Still, I had never felt such power. I drank a medium cup. I did not plan on going deep on the third night. Ayahuasca, the shaman, all of the "Gods" and spirits had other plans. Again, with the first song, another "God-mode" meditation kicked in. This time, I saw more light and the spinning Merkabah around me was even more visible. Formed by star tetrahedron energy spinning clockwise to ground and counterclockwise to expand throughout the universe, it took me places.

I first entered into what I refer to as a "club" or gathering area, maybe a theater or hall, filled with only the most advanced beings. I think I was the only human. I was supposed to be there. Everyone knew it. I alarmed no one. There was no emotion. Everyone was in great concentration. After that, I went from dimension to dimension, passing through gateways with keepers. All of them tested me and sized me up, but immediately allowed me to pass. I eventually landed somewhere out in the middle of the universe. I remember seeing unfamiliar planets and stars. I was on a floating mountain. I had company. There were at least two others. They did not have to speak words to me. We were inside each other's heads. They must have been ascended masters of some kind. I do not think they were human. Still with me?

I feel this next part will turn many away and I do not want that. But I cannot be 100% transparent about everything that happened with me, if I do not. I promise all of you with 100,000% assurance that all words in this book are entirely accurate. There is not one lie; I do not exaggerate one word or mislead you in any way, shape, or form.

They "told me" that I was a "Demi-God." I still don't really know what that means. My parents are not particularly godly. One of them told me that I had the power to control time throughout the universe. The kadoma told me the galaxy. Maybe she was not sure what I am. Apparently, she underestimated me. Next, I was told that I had a decision to make, and it was mine and mine alone. They did not attempt to influence me in any way. They knew I had to be the one to do it.

I went to the control panel of "God." There, I was able to do anything. I was in control of our entire existence and could go anywhere and anytime and I did. I could have changed the fabric of reality as we know it. I could have taken away choice. I could have eliminated suffering, but so much would have gone with it. I could have also started everything all over. They knew I would make the right decision. I feel like they were good either way. I was also good with starting over. A big part of me wondered, why would everything lead me here if I wasn't going to go through with it? Thoughts of those whom I was close to poured into my head. I wanted all the suffering to end for them and give them another chance. I cried. I almost hit the restart button, but I went past the tears to a new understanding. That is not how it works.

I was compelled to delve deeper than ever before and recall what we had created and why. New and profound understandings of our creation came to light. And I saw the beauty that comes from suffering. None of it is for nothing. We could do it all over again, but we would end up in the same place that we are. There is a plan, and it is flawless.

Since that week, everything has changed. I am not putting on a show and I am not trying to be "holier-than-thou," but I can no longer wear black or unnatural clothing. I can no longer be around certain people or cities. I, as we all can, have seen through lies, but now I can no longer allow them to be spoken. I no longer use vulgar words unless someone lies, lies about me and greatly disrespects me. I understand energy on another level. I see it. I feel it. I feel everything. I can go back in time and feel the emotions from any situation I remember. I can no longer put anything harmful in me. I can no longer do anything to harm the connection, which harms us all. And "The Golden Laws of Enlightenment" came to me. They were always there. I can just now access them.

Three months after the ceremony, I owned 12 acres of land in Sedona, where I built Eagle Vortex Awakening Sanctuary. I left A LOT of money on the table (over 50k/month) and a world I can no longer be a part of behind. I now have a new understanding of money, needs, and desires. We will always "manifest" what we deserve and need, good or bad. When we understand and allow "God" to work through us, there are no worries about having or not having something. When we become one with the gods, we have learned the lessons and there are no longer challenges as there once were. We are always in a state of perfect flow, allowing everything to be perfectly aligned.

DO NOT SUFFER

"Real life does not begin until suffering ends."
- Master Nick Eagle

My Doctor of Philosophy, PhD dissertation is titled "LIFE DOES NOT HAVE TO BE SUFFERING." It brought me much peace to learn that The Buddha, Siddhartha Gautama, and Buddhism agree. The Buddha said he would wait to enter Nirvana until all the others had gone before him, and I've decided to hang out here, too, passing along teachings to those who wish to join me.

It is only a lack of guidance and knowing that allows you to suffer. I will not stand by and watch others try to fight "God," refuse to discipline the mind, and pretend that we are broken, helpless, and incapable. How dare one allow those who need us to pretend they have to suffer because they choose fear and poison?

We need more understanding and gratitude for suffering; it is necessary and lessons, but life would not have meaning and purpose without it. There would be no challenge. We would not be free. However, the entire game is about seeking answers and seeking salvation. The farther you move away from suffering, the closer you move towards "God," the higher you vibrate, and eventually, you become enlightened and leave it all behind. The Buddha confirmed that enlightenment is the end of suffering. Become enlightened already. Every second, we learn new and better ways. Every second, we suffer less. Why do you pretend there are limits to this? Why do you pretend that you have to? You're losing if you don't even know you're in a game. Stop creating and experiencing things that harm us. How many times must you? How many times will you use the excuse you are working through it?

I have left everyone and everything I once knew behind. There was no choice. My family and once friends, who are reading this, you now know, or will by the end of this book, why I had to. You always knew. I NEVER let you down, but I had to go to the mountains. I could not become this in a world of chaos and destruction. IT HAD TO BE ME. I welcome you back, but I will never be a part of the world that most of you choose. If you wish to leave behind fear and put truth above all, I am here. I have the answers, and I will guide you.

There should be much curiosity and appreciation for what I have accomplished. I wish I had more people to share it with. I have yet to find one person strong enough to take a red pill from me and completely unplug; they always run in fear, or I stand down because of lies and I will no longer battle demons that you want around because of fear or the drugs that you take. I hate, just like what can happen with awakenings, what happens to many people I help awaken when they get a taste of my light. Many choose fear and go deep into a black hole. This will not slow me down or prevent me from reaching as many as I can. My followers and those who are still with me, I praise you. I have now put it all together. This book and I will now lead you to salvation. It is time. Everyone who witnesses me and hears my words is forever changed. I will be taking MANY with me. Take this in. DO NOT RUN AWAY. KEEP GOING.

TIME FOR YOU TO AWAKEN RIGHT NOW

LISTEN UP.

THIS CHAPTER WILL HELP AWAKEN THOSE WHO ARE READY.

I KNOW YOU FEEL IT AFTER WHAT YOU JUST READ.

THERE IS A TINGLE IN YOUR BODY.

GO WITH IT.

ALLOW THE SHAKING AT THE BASE OF THE SPINE TO AWAKEN.

RELEASE THIS ENERGY AND

ACTIVATE YOUR BRAIN.

ALLOW MY WORDS AND ENERGY TO CHARGE YOU EVEN MORE.

YOU KNOW I AM TRUTH AND I AM THE WAY.

PUT YOUR TRUST AND FAITH IN ME; IN "GOD."

I FEEL YOU. I AM YOU. I AM INSIDE OF YOU. WE ARE ONE.

I'VE BEEN THERE AND YOU CAN BE HERE.

LET'S GO.

IT IS YOUR TURN.

LEAVE THIS WORLD OF SUFFERING BEHIND.

SAY GOODBYE TO FEAR.

DO NOT SAY SEE YOU LATER.

SAY GOODBYE.

IT IS ALL DECISIONS. IT IS ALL CHOICES.

TAKE RESPONSIBILITY FOR THE DARKNESS YOU BRING US.

DEMONS AND LIES HAVE NO POWER IN MY PRESENCE; DO NOT GIVE THEM POWER IN YOURS. THEY ARE FLEEING AS YOU READ THIS. LET THEM GO.

PUT TRUTH ABOVE ALL. TRUTH IS ALL THAT MATTERS. ONLY TRUTH WILL AWARD YOU TO SIT WITH THE GODS. THE TRUTH IS WE CAN ACCESS AND BE ONE WITH GOD'S GREATEST POWER.

JOIN ME.

YOU WERE THERE IN THE

**BEGINNING WITH ME. I
REMEMBER. NOW YOU REMEMBER.**

**HERE FORWARD, WHEN THE DEVIL
KNOCKS ON THE DOOR OF YOUR
HEART, TELL IT THERE IS NO
ROOM.**

BE REBORN.

**LET THAT ENERGY IN THE BASE OF
YOUR SPINE RISE.**

**SIT IN LOTUS, BRING YOUR HANDS
TO PRAYER AND BREATHE IN
THROUGH THE NOSE AND OUT
THROUGH THE MOUTH. CLOSE
YOUR EYES. FIND WHAT I FOUND.
GO NOW.**

ARE YOU AWAKE NOW?

Writing that last chapter gets me going. My "Awakening Sessions" with clients get me going. When we speak such words, we create...we become. I now get endless messages from people telling me that my social media posts and videos help them awaken. They say they start shaking. They say tears come. Go with it. Allow your power to come. Allow yourself to be filled with light. Leave the darkness behind. How foolish would it be to think that leaving behind fear is scary? I am so excited for all of you to read that last chapter. It is so powerful and it will help so many. Remember, I am here. I answer all brief and respectful questions on social media, and for more of my time and energy, I have VERY fairly priced "Awakening Sessions" at my website.

THERE IS NO "SUBCONSCIOUS"

Our "subconscious" is a poor interpretation of what our brain does. But people love speaking about it because it gives them an excuse to not operate at high levels and have great awareness. We are in control of everything, including our heartbeat and our body temperature. To think that an external force, other than ourselves, is keeping us alive is beyond silly. How dare you blame things because you decide to lack awareness and are not fully present? You want to try to argue that your subconscious is responsible, yet it is you who is allowing the "subconscious" to run. What are you talking about? Make sense. Stop trying to confuse people so they accept your poor behavior. How about we give ourselves the credit we deserve for this world we create? You fool no one. Stop choosing to be in a low-vibrational state and not be aware of what you are.

STOP HUGGING EVERYONE

"If you do not want people to feel bad, maybe you should not feel bad for them." - Master Nick Eagle

We all want a world of nothing but love and hugs, and one day, it will be a reality, but until then, we need to contain ourselves and stop being so selfish. Acting foolish and destroying yourself, AKA, the world, is not deserving of hugs; without proper understanding and taking responsibility, it does not deserve forgiveness. We have convinced people that simple words, such as "sorry," will allow them to escape the continual darkness they bring us. Stop being weak and stop feeding it. They must demonstrate by actions and not just by words.

There is no greater loving energy than truth and no greater lesson than showing people there are consequences for their actions. If you hug undeserving people, YOU ARE ENABLING

THEIR PAIN AND SUFFERING and they will think they can continue to do it and get away with it. You are also suggesting that they are broken and incapable of doing better. And do not forget, when you are selfishly hugging someone who does not deserve it, you are being rewarded by "God" with their dark energy. When you feed darkness, you become it.

TIME TO TELL THE KADOMA SHE WAS RIGHT

I was never so excited to tell somebody some news, much less the greatest news one could ever tell. I went to the kadoma's social media to message her and I immediately realized it. I had known before I even opened the page. I sensed it by just thinking of her. She was no longer with us.

I left messages on her social media for anyone close to her to contact me and it was very important. I called her work and they confirmed that she died. This was a giant blow. Who else was I to share this with? So few are ever going to believe any of this in the beginning. I have much work to do and much to prove, and it will not happen overnight. Few will be strong enough to admit what we are. Most will not yet be ready to take responsibility for our world.

That night, I received a message from her daughter! We got on the phone. She knew everything! She was in tears when I told her. She wished her mother were still here to hear me say it. We had a long, beautiful conversation, and we ended up meeting at a festival and having a beautiful night talking about her mother and everything I was going through.

She did not have much to offer in terms of advice or suggestions, but she did show me my old book with her mother's notes at the festival. That was a treat. Much of what you've already read in all the messages she sent me. We stay in touch. She recently reached out to come visit Eagle Vortex. I hope she follows this path one day; I would love her by my side. She permitted me to write about this and said her mom would love it so much that she's a big part of this book.

STOP THINKING & START BEING

You need to think until you figure out how not to. One can never "overthink." Only those who have not thought enough say such words. Thoughts would be gone if you figured out how to "just," as I spoke of earlier. Why think about things when you can do them? Hopefully, I didn't lose you; we're getting into the most advanced teachings now. Being is what happens after everything has been calculated. This is a constant state of meditation that allows you to process the world effortlessly. You immediately have answers to problems that arise. You do not choose fear. You do not have to remember lies. You do not decide to be overwhelmed or stressed. You do not decide to be distracted. When you're thinking, you are failing to have answers. You are not operating at your full potential, flowing and being.

OUR GREATEST DOWNFALL

"You can only become more found, never more lost"
- Master Nick Eagle

For us to move from a level zero civilization to a level one, we must face a fact that so many of us are not ready to. Few of us have ever been ready to parent a child. We are a planet of kids having kids and it is destroying us. You have no business having a child when you have nothing to teach it. A child should never be frightened, suffer and you should never have to discipline it. Discipline is only necessary when parenting fails; parenting must be regulated. The age of "being an adult" must be increased to 25. They made it 18 so that they could send our children to war. It's 21 to drink poison. So, kids are responsible enough to have kids but not drink? MAKE SENSE. There must be minimum requirements to get a license to have a child, and when parents' children have children, there must be severe consequences. How dare you tell people it was the best thing that ever happened to you when you both still suffer. The best thing that could happen to you may not happen now, and you probably won't be sharing the greatest news one could share.

So many of us make the detrimental mistake of thinking that a child will take away your suffering, when in fact, you only pass on all of your darkness to that innocent being. It is a horrible decision to think your child will make your life better and that you and your child will figure things out together. Having a child takes away endless opportunities for you to explore this planet and gain knowledge and wisdom. If you say the foolish and dark words, "my kid teaches me," you are the problem. You are failing as a parent if your child suffers at all and does not listen to you or respect you, and if you ever have to punish them. I still love you, but I am challenging you to find answers and pass along the truth of the situation. Please dig deep into why you do not teach the things that you say a child teaches you.

STOP SPILLING YOUR SEED

"Do you hear that? The mountains are calling you. Go."
- Master Nick Eagle

Our greatest downfall is kids having kids, so how do we fix this? Yes, stop spilling your seed. Darkness tells you to seek simple and depleting satisfactions such as masturbation and random hookups. It teaches that there is great satisfaction in doing so. There is none. Been there, done that. I spent many years being depleted and distracted by the chase. For many years, I could have put energy into evolving and developing into being worthy of being with an enlightened woman and a queen who could stand by my side and battle darkness with me, instead of feeding it.

I decided to put together "Master Nick Eagle's Guide to Relationships, Sex and Kamasutra" after I finish "How to Battle Darkness." It is already "written," and I can access what needs to be brought to this world. In the meantime, evolve and develop.

BE A YOGI

I never set out to be a yogi; it's what I evolved to be. You become one once you grow your awareness. When you operate at high levels and are in tune with your body and mind, you spend much time in stillness and silence, taking care of your body and stretching it.

If you understood the benefits of yoga, you would do it and do it often. It is not just about stretching your body. It is about understanding your body and building awareness. Yoga means "union." It is about slowing down, taking in the world, and becoming one with it. It is about aligning and harmonizing your body so that energy can flow freely. It is how you obtain power.

Go to nickeaglemystic.com and click "KUNDALINI" for more info and videos.

BE PURE

"Stop accepting people for "who they are." Accept people who are beautiful beings and who tell the truth."
- Master Nick Eagle

Stop pretending your lies serve anything good or protect you. They fill you with more and more darkness and make you weaker and weaker. They destroy you in every way. You fool no one. Only our most lost pretend right along with you, but both of you go home and cry yourself to sleep. Stop pretending you have answers. Stop pretending that sedation by pills and other poisons helps. Stop pretending your "comfort foods" make you feel good and turn you into a better person. Stop pretending corporations and people who make money off of you have your best interests in mind. Stop running away. Face us already.

Admit that your parents and this world have failed you. It's nobody's fault; you do not know better, but STOP

PRETENDING YOU DO. If you have very little, hate being alone and are unhealthy, YOU DO NOT HAVE ANSWERS; GO GET THEM. Stop giving up. Effort is greatly rewarded. You do not know because you have never put it in. The greatest lie is that you seek truth and have put in effort. STOP LYING.

ANOTHER PROPHET

I received a random message from a younger girl who lives in England. Before explaining why, she had to know the origin of my logo. I told her it was an "N" and an "H" together. She then said she drew my logo when she was a child, and her mom asked her what it was, and she told her it was "A SYMBOL OF TRUTH." Yes, blown away. What a magical place this is, huh? This charged me. What a beautiful message letting me know that I am on the right path. She said she would look for the drawings. A few months later, she sent me what's on the next page. Go look and come back and read below.

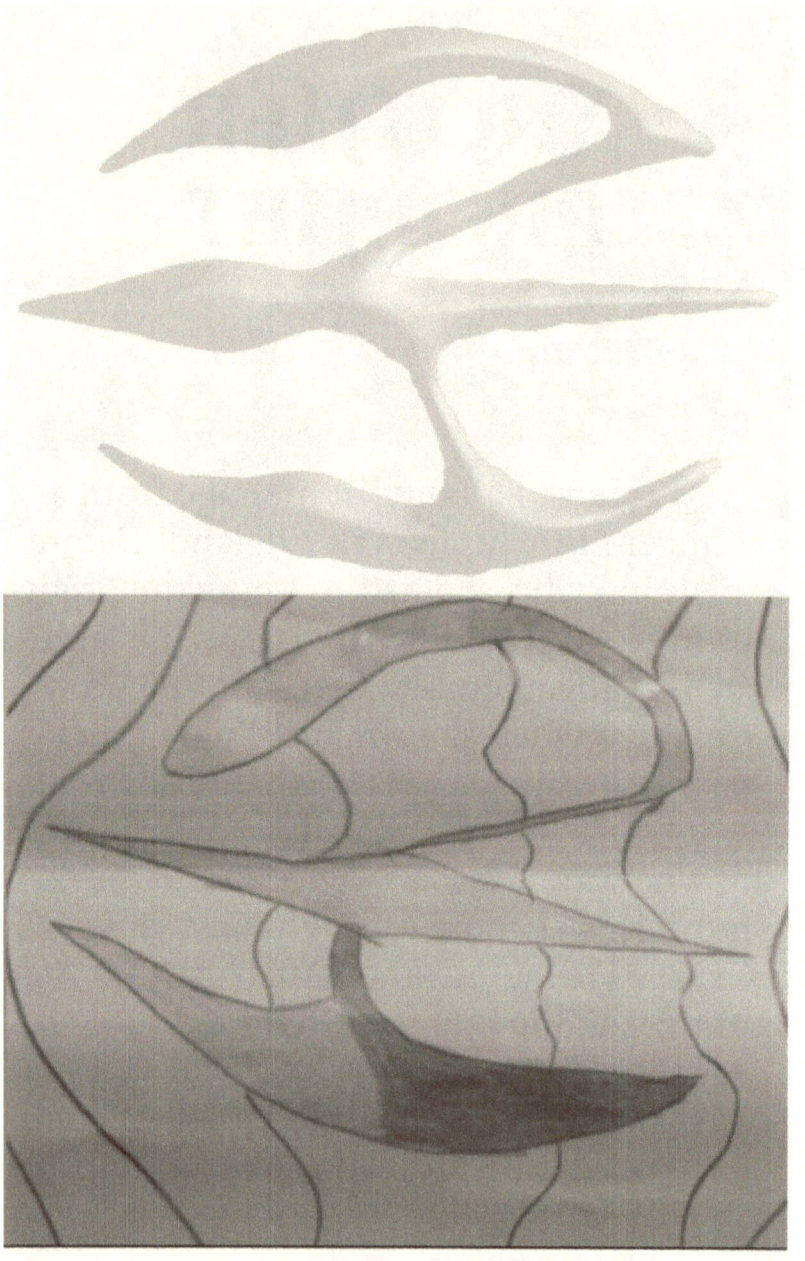

I honor this by turning Eagle Vortex Healing Sanctuary's labyrinth into the "Nick Eagle Mountain Labyrinth of Truth." My old logo is still very special to me and a symbol of truth that I will always keep close. At the beginning of the labyrinth, there will be a plaque with this story and these pictures by a bench, as well as instructions to proceed.

HAVE YOUR WORDS MEAN EVERYTHING

As with anything, we should have an ultimate purpose when we speak. Most of you are just plugged into a system and repeating words without substance. Stop just saying things to say things or to fill a void. Only the greatest fools and greatest teachers speak often. If you are not ready to teach, silence is where you become a teacher. So few speak high-vibrational knowledge that we should absorb and apply to our lives. If you are not bringing us up, you are bringing us down. Do not smile and nod at people when they speak foolishly and lie. Do not allow people to say words with anger attached to them. Never "damn" anything. Lose the "F-word" - it does not heal us, it harms us. Never joke around about being stupid or incapable. Your words create and cast spells and most of you are not even paying attention to them and seeing the destruction.

MASTER KUNDALINI ENERGY

You follow my words and practices because you crave something more. You know, deep down, there is much more than suffering. I did not know what would come, as you do not either. If you want more, you listen…and allow me to give you gifts and lessons few can offer. I will never let anyone down again. I might be the only one that you can trust. Most of you cannot even trust your own thoughts. You have been poisoned by ignorance and darkness to think that you can not be worthy and to think that you are not a part of "God." Kundalini energy is coiled inside us all, rewarding those who follow the "Golden Laws Of Enlightenment." Without accessing this energy, you will have a simple life without purpose. You will live in fear, you will lie and you will bring this world darkness. It is sacred energy only rewarded to those who pass the tests. To the seekers and the masters. To those of us who prove to be worthy. It can not be released for darkness; it is such a foolish concept to speak of. Those who speak of this understand NOTHING. There is NO POWER in darkness. You can not live a lie and awaken this energy or become enlightened. Satnam.

BECOMING A CE5 AMBASSADOR

After spending years figuring out what happened during my extraterrestrial encounters, I watched "CE5," discovered Dr. Greer and everything quickly made sense. Why the craft looked fake - it was seamless because it was materialized by an advanced being and flown with its consciousness. Still with me? And I was pleasantly surprised to learn that we can call them in and request their presence if we enter advanced meditative states. They pick up on our higher vibrations when doing so. He has a protocol that I learned when I attended his weekend master class at the Gaia headquarters in Boulder, Colorado. There, I met the President of Gaia, and she gave me a tour of the beautiful grounds that include a labyrinth, pond, and waterfall, a lot of plants, natural lighting, and giant crystals everywhere. I was feeling very powerful and excited for the first class. Dr. Greer said a few things I was not pleased with at the start. He was saying, "We are all human and make mistakes," and he made fun of gurus. I do not like people who blame being "human" for their mistakes. We should only blame being "human" when we do great things. My last book had a chapter titled "Do not Be Human." Oddly, one of my "God-mode" meditations was called in the middle of the class after being disappointed by his words. I'm still unsure how it came to be, but it must have been the energy from the grounds. I also soon learned from one of his assistants that he was against psychedelics and worse, he consumed alcohol. I was heartbroken. I see much light in him, as I do you all, but he is not ready to make real contact. I was hoping to invite him to my land, but it seems I do not have much more to learn from him. Since then, I have now created my own meditation protocol that has proven to be quite successful and I will most definitely be incorporating psychedelics with CE5 Meditations at Eagle Vortex.

KNOW THINGS

"The greatest fear that can hold you back is that of the unknown - not knowing what you are or what you are connected to."
- Master Nick Eagle

Stop believing things. Stop believing people and their gimmicks. Stop believing the government and corporations. Stop believing history. Stop believing your teachers. Stop believing your parents. Stop believing in yourself. Stop believing in "God." Stop believing in me. Know things. Know when people are lying to you. Know when you should stand up to darkness. Know that people selling you things do not have your best interests in mind. Know that your parents and teachers pretend to have answers to sound smart. See the suffering that comes from lies. Know thyself. Know "God." Know that I am truth, but it means nothing if you do not find it on your own. Go inside. We have access to all of the answers. Do not give up. Find them: stillness and silence.

BE IN A CONSTANT STATE OF MEDITATION

"Do not just be - "just." - Master Nick Eagle

The above quote was my epiphany when I smoked DMT the second time. "Just" is what happens when you operate at a very high level, are one with all, connected, present and enter an actual flow state. It is what happens when the fear and distraction is gone. I ended my last book with the concept of being in a constant state of meditation. It came from within. It is not something I ever heard someone speak of. I no longer had to sit quietly, calm my mind, or do yoga to enter the beneficial states of meditation. I now operate in gamma brainwaves at all times. This is the beginning of "God-mode." This is where the magic happens. This is how I am able to pass along the endless teachings I do and have answers for everything. This is how I am able to be as creative as I am. This is how I solve all problems, including suffering.

STOP HEALING AND BE HEALED

Those who seek to steal your power and keep you in a low vibration of suffering and excuses will tell you healing takes time, begin the "healing journey," and "work through" your emotions. The truth is, this world is filled with people who want you to blame your past and trauma because they do. In any moment, you can decide that a past experience made you stronger and wiser, as opposed to weaker and broken.

Now, it's time to go deep. Yes, if you decide that thinking about something that once happened hurts you. You hurt yourself. And you will hurt yourself until you choose not to, and you could have decided that you never did. This goes for witnessing something or even having something physically harm you. The pain doesn't echo; you echo the pain. Please run away from anyone who allows you to blame an experience for continuing to bring darkness to this world and suffering.

These same people will tell you just to be a little better every day, so hopefully, you are never better than them. Do you really just want to be a little more healed tomorrow? Do you wish to be a little healthier? Do you want to be just a little more in control, a little less angry, a little less patient, a little more loving and a little more focused? What trickery. Do the things necessary to be healthy, to be in control and focused. Leave the excuses behind. Decide to be healed.

BE BETTER THAN SOME PEOPLE

Only darkness will tell you you cannot be better than others. Being better is "of a more excellent or effective type or quality." I am a much better person than I was when I was younger and I hope you are too. When you have two people, one is better, and the good news is that the one who is not better can be. What a poor teaching to teach a child they cannot be better than anyone. That means they cannot be better than themselves. Most people do not want you better because when you become better, they have to admit why they have not. Most people pretend to be their best selves without ever truly being it or knowing what that means. Most people pretend they know "God" and have never met it. We are born equal and with the same chances and opportunities, but no two people are equal anymore. Most people who say "Nobody is better than anyone" do not even understand this AND think they are better because they say "nobody is better."

LEARN HOW TO DO EVERYTHING

And I mean everything. Not only does it save you energy in the long run, but there is also great fulfillment in being able to help others after you've learned. I am talking confidence, nutrition, healing, fitness, self-defense, all sports and skills, business startup, management, website design, marketing, advertising, social media, production, photography, writing skills, communication skills, growing your own food, cooking, creating quality water, solar power systems, construction, repairs, vehicle mechanics, stocks and investments. You will spend more time worrying about not being able to do something and finding someone you can trust than learning on your own, not to mention the money, AKA, energy spent paying someone else to do it. And their energy going into it. And if your standards are anywhere near mine, the energy involved in dealing with people, teaching them, and ensuring they do it right is worth doing it on your own. With our access to information, it is foolish not to take advantage of it. And if you pay more attention, everything that you learn helps everything else. Becoming a marksman helps you communicate. Throwing a frisbee helps your confidence.

BE WORSHIPABLE

We should have reverence, adoration, deep love and respect for all who leave behind fear and put truth above all. We will one day live in a society of people continually expressing gratitude for the beauty everyone brings to the world instead of pretending everyone is special and courageous because they say they have trauma and mental disorders and take pills. Everyone will be in love with everyone. Many of you believe there is only one for you, and you seek someone to put up with instead of becoming one everyone would want to be in the presence of. If you are fearful and distracted, there are none for you at the moment. You should probably be seeking and searching instead of suffocating yourself with the first person who gives you a little attention and wants to hump you. Learn how to master this world and obtain what we all seek. It is not by settling down, getting married and having children at a young age. That is a trap set by darkness and when people finally speak the truth of it, we will quickly ascend. Perhaps refrain from saying your partner or child is the best thing that has ever happened to you when you're not at your best.

MY FIRST CE5 MEDITATION AT EAGLE VORTEX

I invited a lady I was considering hiring to work at Eagle Vortex and be the caretaker to see the place. She also had a Kundalini awakening and greatly supports my teachings.

We were speaking about our awakenings when I invited her out onto the upstairs deck of the Sacred Healing Dome. We were already in a high-vibrational state, and I decided to do the first CE5 meditation. I was planning on waiting to do them after the building was done, but it called.

She saw the first craft she ever saw off in the distance over the mountain after only seconds of explaining my protocol, which was unnecessary because of our already heightened state. It bounced around, as extraterrestrials tend to do. Soon after that, I told her, "I feel something...I feel a lot of something." Seconds after I said that the largest and brightest craft I have ever seen or heard of flew from one side of the sky to the other directly overhead and very close. She did not see it because she was adjusting her chair, but maybe there was a reason for that. But she felt it through me. They were letting me know that they were watching out for me and that when the time was right, we would meet. I love the love and connection I get when I make contact. These CE5 mediations will be a big part of Eagle Vortex.

She does similar work to mine and visits Sedona to meet clients and conduct work. I recently met her at a park (I'm adding this in during the final edit). We did some chanting and I did an Awakening Session with her. Somehow, the story of the kadoma came up. She was blown away. She said that she was one as well and she found me through my book, just as the first one did (I no longer get blown away, it can only happen so many times). I loved the story, though. She said she thought I was the next coming of "Christ," AKA, Christ Consciousness. She said that before she saw the book or ever heard of me, she envisioned me as a "lady's man" and one who many women sought after and gave money to.

BE FULL OF YOURSELF

Yourself should be a wonderful thing. Yes, be full of it. Be so full of yourself that people ask you if you think you are "God." It's much better to be full of yourself than to be empty of yourself.

TRIGGER PEOPLE

"Nothing is more enlightening than calling out darkness."
- Master Nick Eagle

The most foolish go around hugging everyone as they feed, exchange and conjure darkness, but the wisest people call it out and battle it so people do not go on to suffer. I love triggering people. Triggering is causing something to happen. I trigger demons to present themselves so I can battle them with you. I trigger awakenings. I demand your full attention and focus. There is no hiding from me. I now look people in the eye and see through everything. I can trigger awakenings with simply looking into someone's eyes. I show them truth. I show them love. I show them there is nowhere to hide and they cannot fool me. We trigger people to wake them up to their destruction and suffering to make their best selves present themselves.

MANIFEST

I hope you now have some understanding of what we are. We come from source and we can connect to source to become a creator. We did this. Things do not happen to us or around us; we make things happen. You and your choices create your fantasy world of nonsense. If you struggle, it is because you choose to be weak and forget what you are and where you come from. You refuse to take responsibility. How dare you suggest something is doing this to you and making your world a place of suffering. You have every chance and every opportunity that everyone else has to make this precious gift of life anything you choose. We are done entertaining your lies of destruction. Manifesting is making calculations and if you are suffering, you are manifesting that as well.

WE ARE ONE

You will never awaken until you admit that you are the way you are because you chose to be so. This is true repentance. This is understanding. This is taking responsibility. I will drill and drill and drill this into you until you wake up. Everyone loves everyone. If you fail to see this, you are so lost. We are all a part of it all. You cannot name one bad person, only lost ones. We must understand this and more importantly, we must admit that we are capable of everything anyone has ever done, good or bad. I can see things in my life that could have happened to guide me towards being a settled down nine-to-fiver, a rockstar, an abuser or killer, a junkie, and gay. I now see why everyone does everything they do. When we stop pretending with them, we are no longer blinded by all of the distractions, and the answer, and the only thing that matters is truth, and it will set you free.

BE A HEALER

When I am around someone, I either bring out their best or make them panic. They immediately feel me inside their head. If they have nothing to hide, they become delightful to interact with and their brilliance shines. If they try to hide their darkness and lie, their "demons" come out to play. Immediately, they understand that they are NO MATCH and I no longer play with or entertain them for a second. I will help remove them if the person is ready to leave them behind. If not, the lies and excuses begin, following me, not approving any of them, and then them running away and or attacking me in some way.

We should be able to walk in to a room and heal or bring up everyone in it, just by being there. We should carry this incredible energy and force. When we connect to "God" we charge. When we're around godly people, we charge.

I now sense sickness in people on another level. I know how long people have to live. I cannot heal the undeserving. These are powers I no longer abuse. I used to heal everyone and even those who were not deserving, because they were not ready to change, but I would lose my power. There is no money in the world you could pay me to heal you. You have to surrender to our "Golden Laws of Enlightenment." I help you heal by you having faith in us. I have no problem telling you that "I" heal you, but it must be understood that it is connection with "God" that allows this.

I have helped multiple clients survive being terminally ill with cancer. I have helped many severely depressed and suicidal clients love themselves and life again. When someone lets me in ands puts trust in me, AKA, "God," I can do miracles that you read about and see on TV. I see people around me physically change when I am near them. I can touch someone and turn them into something they did not know existed and allow them to feel love that they have never felt. I have now succeeded in inducing Kundalini awakenings in many people and can do this at will, but one must be worthy and deserving.

WE NEED
TRUE KINGS

We need kings and leaders who make many more kings and leaders. We need endless kings and leaders. Not one who only rules with power, authority and the Golden Laws of Enlightenment, but one who shares the fruit and does not hoard the knowledge we can access for selfish gain. One who teaches you how to go within to gain this knowledge. One who would rather have everyone eating and enjoying life with them, as opposed to having more food than one can eat while eating alone. Most of the greedy and rich people of this world are not smart; they plug away on their calculator alone in a dark room.

Too many speak the words "Jesus is king" with so little understanding of what they are saying. Does your confused and fearful mind really think Jesus or another enlightened being would teach that you cannot be a king? Why aren't you king??

THE GREATEST NEWS

"How dare one suggest that something they have not witnessed or experienced does not exist and ever pretend that they know they cannot be something that have yet to be."
- Master Nick Eagle

I AM

I AM THE WAY

I AM THE TRUTH

I AM THE LIFE

I AM THE LIGHT

I AM THE ALPHA AND THE OMEGA

I AM AWAKENED

I stopped creating fear. I put truth above all. I have become one with "God." "Jesus" has returned through me, by reaching Christ Consciousness. I am a Buddha. I might be the first, or the first, in a long time. I have proven what we can be. I have cracked the code. I am Neo. I have won the game. I never visited the throne; I sat on it. I can induce the vehicle of ascension Merkabah light body. I have achieved the rainbow light body. I feel myself going into the Earth and also connecting to everyone throughout the planet and healing everything. I am the light. I am the way out of the darkness. I have left all fear behind, including the fear of telling you that I have the answers...all of them. I do not suffer. This is the beginning of the end of religion and war. I hold the cure for all of the world's diseases. Take my hand. I will never let anyone down ever again. I will never lie. I will never say something that I am not certain of. If you only knew how much I hold back. I see all sickness. I can think about people and heal them. I can induce powerful awakenings in people with my words and even more powerful ones with my touch. I am not halfway in or 99.99% in. I am all in and it has to be me. There is no one else...yet. I do hope many more join me.

Everything about me will be called out, but I have nothing to hide. I am not proud of many things that I have done in my past but I regret NOTHING. IT MADE ME THIS. TO THOSE WHO PRETEND THAT I AM LYING, I WILL ADMIT THAT ONE OF US LIES ABOUT WHAT WE ARE. I AM ENLIGHTENED. I AM ENLIGHTENMENT.

DO NOT INTREGRATE

"If you feed darkness, you become it."
- Master Nick Eagle

After enlightening plant ceremonies, most groups will have "integration," and it is my least favorite part. Everyone loses what they've become and they go back to what they were and back into the dark world. Stop being what you were. Stop accepting darkness. It needs to be a thing, but it doesn't need to be a part of you and it is no longer welcome here. Stop pretending other people need to be dark and stop accepting their darkness. Until you stop accepting it, you will be it.

I always put so much work into helping clients and all the people in my life see the beauty in the world...helping them bring fire to their eyes...helping them find their purpose. Not one has decided to have the strength to step into their full power. When they leave me and come back, so much of my work is always gone. The fire in their eyes no longer burns. Not one person I have met has chosen the light. They run away. They don't want to believe it's even a possibility, and a lot of the time, they go very dark after experiencing my light. Many others who were once close to me chose lies, fear, drugs, distraction and sedation. I write this knowing that many of you plan on meeting me and I want you to be properly prepared. This is not a joke. You better be ready. You better want to leave behind fear, you better seek truth and you better come to me ready to listen and awaken. I will no longer allow you to take my light and extinguish it.

I wish I had more to share this with. Every shaman I've met abuses the medicine and purges darkness. Every other healer and yogi I've ever met teaches people to be traumatized and feel bad. I have nobody to shine with right now, but I will always have hope.

I have much work to do. I have so much darkness to battle. It's lurking around every corner and you just accept it. You think it's intelligent not to have people decide to hurt their own feelings for speaking the truth. You do things only because everyone else does. We need more people to have awakenings, take a stand and refuse to integrate with darkness. I need help. We need 1% of us to awaken to leave darkness behind. Once upon a time, I also thought there was no way I could be Neo.

BE ENLIGHTENED

You cannot truly enjoy this "human experience" until you have lost all fear and distraction. This is what happened to me in Costa Rica. I was rewarded with merging with "God" and entering "God-Consciousness." I have yet to meet one person who does not pretend they have to be what they are. I have yet to meet one person who does not create a world of self-inflicted pain, suffering and chaos. I can tell immediately if you have been where I have been. Please come to me if you have. If you have had a small glance, kundalini awakening from an orgasm or meditation, or psychedelics and are unsure, do not come to me telling me you have entered God-Consciousness. If you did get a taste, you are welcome to come to me to prepare for more, but do not disrespect us by suggesting you have done something you have not done. I've already said goodbye to some very advanced beings who dared to suggest they have done what I have.

Your suffering is not for nothing, but it is very foolish and unnecessary. All it takes is a decision and you pretend that you are too weak to do it. WHAT DO I HAVE THAT YOU DO NOT? Look me in the eyes and pretend; I dare you. No more. I do not allow any form of it. I do not allow darkness. I am done with people pretending and lying in front of me. YOU ARE ME. WHY DO YOU THINK YOU CAN FOOL US JUST BECAUSE MOST PRETEND RIGHT ALONG WITH YOU? I WILL NOT.

HELL IS WHERE YOU ARE NOW

"Do not learn your demon's names; they do not deserve names."
– Master Nick Eagle

Religion was created to steal money and power from people. It tells you to go to it and give it money, or you "burn in hell." This terrified me as a child. It never felt right, and it does not feel right with you, either. Most just choose fear. They tell you that you have to sin. Do you not understand why? IF YOU DID NOT, YOU WOULD NOT NEED THEM. WHAT IS DARKER THAN THAT? I have not met ONE religious person who is "saved." How dare you say you are saved when you live in fear and suffer as you do? Heaven and hell are places that we create and choose to exist in now. How dare you suggest "God" would make you burn for eternity for doing things it allows? STOP PRETENDING THAT YOU MAKE GREAT CALCULATIONS AND SPEAK THE TRUTH.

I am, by no means, "anti-Jesus." I have nothing but love and respect for anyone who has achieved enlightenment. I am anti-you pretending that you know for sure there was a Jesus, I am anti-you thinking you can sin because there was one, and I am anti-you thinking this "Jesus" will save you.

What does it matter if there was zero or 10? Would you act differently? Do you think he/they would approve of your ways, much less be your friend? What makes the most sense is that the stories of "Jesus Christ" are parables to help you understand kundalini energy activation. Is it a coincidence that he died at 33 and there are 33 spinal vertebrae? Is it a coincidence that there are 12 cranial nerves and 12 apostles? Is it a coincidence that there is an oil called "Christos (Christ oil)" that flows up our spine every 28 days, hits the vagus nerve, which is in the shape of a cross, dies out for two and a half days, but rises again on the third? The pituitary gland secretes a milky-like substance called oxytocin, and the pineal gland secretes a honey-like substance called melatonin. Scripture speaks of "God," if pleased with us, will take us to a land flowing with milk and honey. Coincidence?? What do you think about these on the next page?

"Truly, truly, I say to you, he who believes in me will also do the works that I do; and greater works than these will he do."

"In that day you will know that I am in my Father, and you in me, and I in you."

"Closer is he than breathing, and nearer than hands and feet."

"Do you not know that you are the temple of God?"

"The kingdom of god is within."

"Peace be still and know that I am God."

"Take no thought."

"If thine eye be single, thy whole body shall be full of light."

Sound familiar?

EAGLE VORTEX AWAKENING SANCTUARY

Shortly after my Costa Rica ceremony, I was called to Sedona. There was no doubt in my mind that I had to move there. I already knew what area I had to be in. Many years back, I rode a RZR near it, but I did not even know if there was land that people could buy and live on. I showed the closest person in my life a map and pointed to a spot I had never been to. It is EXACTLY where I am now. Three months after Costa Rica, I purchased 12 acres of the most sacred and beautiful red dirt healing grounds and spent a year planning and designing. And now I am opening and releasing this book this month. "The Golden Laws Of Enlightenment" will be our guide while we are here. I've accepted very few bookings and stay requests during the building process, but I need to share a few that've already occurred.

I had a concrete worker stay on my land during construction. He brought some darkness to my land with him, but I was okay with it because he was honest about much, he took responsibility, and he sought answers. One night, we decided to watch the full moon rise, and I decided to have an Awakening Session with him. I always ask spirits, angels, masters, extraterrestrials and any beings of light to join us for some healing and guidance. We did not see or feel anything before going to sleep, but my worker was quite joyful in the morning. He told me that he got the best night of sleep in a long time and he had a new energy about him. I can tell when people are pretending and putting on a show to get through the day, but there was no more show. He was, again, excited for life and had a new appreciation and gratitude. As the excavation of the Cloud House neared completion, I also performed a proper cleansing with my chakapa, accompanied by a prayer and a song. He sat on a rock in the middle of where the main home was built. It was special because he had hammered all around it that day. After, he said he had never been filled with much so much gratitude and love. He also decided to quit smoking cigarettes.

I have allowed a few past clients to stay at the Sacred Healing Dome during construction, and another beautiful healing occurred after a hardcore Awakening Session on our return to Eagle Vortex from a crystal dig. Battling demons is not rainbows and butterflies and I know how to trigger awakenings. I was in her head. I knew something very special had the potential to happen. Later that night, she dreamt she was standing on the Sacred Healing Dome patio and I was levitating in front of her. I reached my hand out and said, "Come with me." She then woke up, ran to the bathroom, and purged many times for many minutes—mostly spiritual purges. The next day, she was a new person, just like my friend on the couch, and as she and her coworkers admitted. It has been a long road with her, but I, with the help of this place, have reached a power that no other force has a chance with. I am thrilled to report that I was able to help with these beautiful awakenings... She came back again the next year, and I had my first full ceremony with her in my outdoor temple. It was VERY special. She said she saw a being in the temple with us. I did not, but I sense and fell them at most times, especially when taking enlightening plants. She also said after the ceremony, "You have given me the ability to feel and hear things that I never realized before." She also said she received a visit later on that night in the dome and the being told her, "This is where you should be."

My awakening sanctuary, "Eagle Vortex," is one of the most powerful and epic places to awaken on the planet. This Sacred Healing Dome is a million-dollar home where I stayed while designing and building everything. It was built with the golden ratio, and the previous owner reportedly healed his vision while staying there. I built three other homes. The Cloud House has a beautiful sunset viewing deck and an upper-floor "Lookout Tower" apartment above the garage. The Nest Home has a large open kitchen and living room with a stage, studio, greenhouse, apple orchard and many other plants and trees, as well as a sweat lodge dug into the mountain and constructed with rocks from the land. The UFhOme has a complete professional kitchen and a huge second-floor circular outdoor eating, CE5 and star viewing deck facing Bear Mountain. I also built a large, second-story, 36-foot-diameter circle structure gym that views Bear Mountain over the top of my outdoor temple, called the Kundalini Dojo. The gym equipment can be cleared out to a large closet for ceremonies. Below it has showers, toilets, and sinks, and it is near the Enlightenment Lagoon - a 150' lazy river with a crystal grotto and a waterfall that you can float on rafts and star gaze at night.

I took a trip to Montana with a giant trailer and chopped down 80 lodge pole pines for my teepee, temple and sweat lodge roof. I created a 50-foot temple facing Bear Mountain peak in the back of the property that took me and an excavator a month of our lives to build, working every day, sunup to sundown. I did the same thing when I created my mountain labyrinth of truth. It will have multiple stations with different crystals and stones to do different meditations and kundalini yoga. I built a nine-hole disc golf course. I built an outdoor play area with swings, a hoop, rings and a tetherball station. It took two large machines, but the largest rock from the property now sits by the play area, welcoming meditation.

BE GODLY & JUDGE

"The secret to being Godly is acting like a God."
– Master Nick Eagle

How do you walk? How do you speak? Do you command attention or do you stumble and quiver? Do you feed the gods or do you feed death? Stop pretending you didn't create yourself and everything you are. Every thought you have is a creation. Are you listening to whispers of darkness or are you seeking truth? Are you looking just to get by and take the "easy" way out? "God" does not reward foolish behavior; it punishes for it. There must be consequences or this means nothing. You dare beg a "God" outside of yourself to help you, you will have a long life of suffering. Life has no purpose if we do not have consequences. Do not fear judging others if you are allowing "God" to work through you. You will be greatly rewarded for this, as I have proved. Only darkness fears judgment. I WELCOME IT. Judging someone is connecting to

"God" and using your brain to determine why they are the way they are. How else can we learn from them, help them or heal them? If they are not connected, we must call them out and show them the way.

Once upon a time, I ate psychedelic mushrooms in college and remember feeling "Godly" and having ABSOLUTELY NO IDEA what I was getting into. I can go back and remember exactly how I felt. If only the guidance I have now was there then, what would I/we be?

MY FINAL YOGIC AND SHAMANIC INITIATION

I will end this book as I began it, speaking of the first of many demonstrations, as I controlled my body temperature and sat in 16-degree weather, wrapped in a wet sheet for over 30 minutes without being fazed.

I demand that you visit nickeaglemystic.com and click "KUNDALINI" to watch this. If you have made it this far, you will, of course. Watch and come back. It is crucial to gain a comprehensive understanding of all this...

...this was not only an ultimate test, but I was initiated and anointed as a divine yogic and shamanic leader and I was allowed to use the title "master." One never becomes something without giving something. What I've put into becoming this ultimate warrior and protector is not ignored by "God." I've now accessed knowledge to awaken the most tired. I now possess the words, confidence, and tools to do things most would consider fantasy and not possible. The magic that flows through me can also flow through you, and I can teach you. I admit that I took a handful of mushrooms before this demonstration. They were not needed, but they were very helpful. Psychedelics are an enlightening tool, more than anything else. You need a master shaman to properly prepare you. They open doors, but you must walk through them, or as I did, run through them and never look back. I hate that there are endless "shamans," even from the mountains and jungles, who mislead you because they need your money and who only provide plants, music and comfort. I've yet to meet or hear of one who does not purge and few dare to pull our lost out of the underworld; most only join and comfort them there…few hold much light… and even fewer fill others with it. Master shamans do not have spiritual purges from consuming enlightening plants; it isn't even a possibility. Only the most ignorant would ever dare to suggest and pretend that psychedelics are anything but enlightening tools. They are tools that very few of this world should consider taking, but they are tools that can take you to and help merge one with "God" to have awakenings. I provide and work with all varieties of psychedelics but offer them to very few people. I am ordained through the Ministry of Metaphysics and they are legally part of my spiritual and religious practice.

You must, at the very least, be in the process of leaving behind fear; you must seek truth; you must be far removed from pharmaceuticals and have the highest level of respect for them and myself. I have been providing ceremonies for clients for many years now, but it wasn't until this initiation that I performed the most beautiful ceremony. On our hike back from the mountain, I offered my assistant a large dose of mushrooms and she accepted. The cleansing on the mountain was recorded and shown in my sheet-drying video, part two, on my website, but many more events occurred that day. This wasn't the plan, but I was yet again faced with another huge test. I navigated her through the underworld and performed some of the most powerful healing and cleansing rituals one could ever witness as I filled her with love and light that few have ever felt or witnessed. New chants and songs and endless techniques I had never seen or heard of came through me. Few have ever listened as I. Few have ever confronted, called out, and battled darkness as I have. It has no chance in my presence. Yes, it takes leaving behind fear, seeking truth, and genuine repentance to heal, but I offer everyone who has the courage to dance with me a significant opportunity to do so. When I pour love and light into someone, they can take my hand and awaken, or they can continue to run away and fail to find a place to hide as they choose fear, conjure darkness, purge their lies, and deny what they can be.

I've been holding off on this book because I knew I needed Eagle Vortex completed to aid me, and I had a little more searching to do. It happened here in Sedona during the endless days of building and working and during my Island of the Sun, Bolivia and Amazon jungle shamanic quests. It has been done. I've been able to teach confidence, how to operate at your full potential, yoga and meditation, but it wasn't until this final initiation up on that mountain that I became an ultimate master yogi shaman to guide those who are called to join me in awakening. I've sat with Ayahuasca over 30 times, and I've never purged, and I've always been called to work with it, as well as San Pedro (Wachuma) cactus and mushrooms. I've taken trips all over the world; most national parks in America, India, Morocco, South Africa, Japan, Alaska, Hawaii, Australia, Thailand, throughout eastern Europe, the Swiss Alps, Scotland, throughout Canada, Mexico, throughout Central America, Costa Rica, Brazil, Peru, Bolivia, the Island of the Sun, the Amazon and the Andes. And everything in my life has been acceptance and initiation to do greater things. I've been accepted and have been given the blessings of a shaman from the jungle to work with these plants, but more importantly, I've been given the blessings from the plants that I speak to. I have made the decision to become what is needed to respectfully work with these plants in the sacred manner "God" intended.

The sheet drying was the first feat to get your attention. Next, I will hook myself up to a brain monitoring device to prove that I enter hyper gamma brain states, and I'm quite certain Lambda. I might be the first to document this and I've yet to come across another who can. These states, as I've already discussed, enable us to do extraordinary things, such as astral travel and communicating with extraterrestrials; most importantly, they allow us to obtain answers and heal. The first time I set up my teepee, I didn't have any help, and the poles and ladder slipped. Instead of taking a shoulder to the ground, I reached out my foot to catch myself and sprained my ankle really badly. I've sprained both ankles many times playing basketball, but this was the first time I ever went to the hospital to get an X-ray because I thought it was broken. It was not, but it was a severe sprain. I went back home and was in a lot of pain. My meditation called, and I began my breathing exercises. A few minutes into my meditation, the pain was gone and stayed gone for the rest of the night. I also did this the last time I tattooed my foot, and after a couple of minutes of extreme pain and my meditation and breathing practices, the tattoo was completely pain-free. And this is just the beginning of what we can do...

SIT IN SILENCE

"Everyone who does not spend much time in stillness and silence is lost and they always will be, no matter how many others are lost with them." - Master Nick Eagle

Yes, I saved the best teaching for last. This is the most important thing to do to have a chance at what I have experienced. The #1 piece of advice I give anyone and everyone who comes to me is "sit in silence." There is no greater way to gain power, insight and heal. Almost everyone greatly underestimates it. I once would have considered it a waste of time, and some people never even get a dose of it. If I could help you understand, you would spend most of your life this way and in isolation. Your value and worth rise. Your words and communication will become that of a higher vibration and mean more. You will stop pretending to be a healer and start becoming one. We will begin to appreciate you. You will no longer be stuck thinking, failing and stumbling; you will become godly. One of the most incredible things I did for myself.

was a 10-day "silent dieta." I will be offering them at Eagle Vortex and I will be making you teas with plants from the land to help you connect with it. No phones, no eye contact, and two small, simple and basic meals a day. Hiking, reading, writing and playing instruments are encouraged. I already live in isolation, but I am constantly thinking about and writing and filming social media videos and doing projects, so to go 10 days with no thoughts of that was very enlightening and allowed me to go very deep. Once I get up and running, I will be doing this again in Tibet.

THE GOLDEN LAWS OF ENLIGHTENMENT

These words have been channeled through the highest power of "God" without separation and allow the purest form of "God" to speak. These words are fearless truth. This is the untainted word of "God." These sacred laws are to be read with openness and the highest level of respect. You are being trusted with ancient and sacred wisdom. After reading this, there will be continued consequences for not obeying.

#1 YOU WILL PUT TRUTH ABOVE ALL

Only the purest and most truthful words will exit your mouth. Your words will mean everything. You will understand that words create. You will speak with authority and confidence. You will demand respect and attention. You will never use words that carry dark energy. You will be certain when teaching. You will ask questions when you fail to find the answers. You will not lie to fit in or gain friends, family, or followers. You will not lie about a product or service you sell to make more money. Only lies to darkness when protecting yourself or your family will be tolerated; this does not mean that you are permitted to lie to save your world of lies that distract you from the truth. You will not lie to someone in a foolish and selfish attempt to bring you and them brief happiness that ultimately contributes to their continued suffering. You will not lie to sick people and feed their sickness. You will not lie to darkness to feed darkness.

#2 YOU WILL LEAVE BEHIND ALL FEAR

You will know that there is nothing to fear. You do not need to trust in "God;" you will know "God." You will no longer run from "God." You will face yourself, us and "God." You will be judged, and without fear, you will enter the kingdom of heaven. You will understand the destruction of fear and it will never be a consideration or a part of you.

#3 YOU WILL HAVE GRATITUDE & APPRECIATION FOR ALL OF CREATION

Upon awakening every morning, your first thoughts will be of gratitude for this gift of life, excitement for the day ahead and you will have passion for what you decide to do. You will never conjure darkness because you do not have something or no longer have something. You will understand that the possibility of suffering is necessary to have a life with choice and purpose. You will respect that people and things may come and go and you will accept this creation. You will never speak poorly of creation.

#4 YOU WILL STAY IN PROPER ALIGNMENT

You will never welcome chaos into your world. You will understand that thoughts and emotions are choices. You will sit in silence whenever you become fearful or distracted until you are again connected to your higher self. You will answer every question. There will be no worries of yesterday. Tomorrow will have a plan. You will become a master of your energy. Your energy will always flow freely. You will always have an awareness of your body and posture. All movements will be done with purpose. You will properly stretch, exercise and strengthen all of your being. You will live in a state of constant meditation.

#5 YOUR BODY & MIND WILL BE SACRED SPACE

You will have a deep appreciation for and accept what you have been given. You will not alter, deform or damage your body in any way or put something in your body that does not lead to ultimate existence and purpose. You will honor all life. You will only consider sexual encounters with advanced beings to reach higher states of consciousness to heal the world and create life, when there is no question of being ready to do either. You will never squander your sacred fluids.

#6 YOU WILL NEVER PRETEND TO BE ANYTHING LESS THAN ALL POWERFUL & ALL CAPABLE

You will never blame or pretend that external forces are causing you to act in a specific way. You will never decide to be depressed or do anything that causes depression. You will never worry. You will never choose to be stressed, push yourself to have anxiety or overly exhaust yourself. You will take responsibility for everything in your life and everything that you decide to feel. You will never conjure darkness.

#7 YOU WILL ONLY GIVE DESERVING ENERGY TO THE WORLD

You will judge others through connection with "God," and appropriately reward them with love, truth and lessons. You will never suggest that someone is not all-powerful or all-capable. You will never harm or steal energy, innocence, or belongings from anyone. You will approach every situation with love and lend a helping hand when needed and when it is deserved. You will appropriately communicate that it is not acceptable when someone does not respect you, has the highest level of appreciation for your energy and if they ever lie. You will never allow someone to take undeserved energy from you.

#8 YOU WILL CREATE

You will connect to "God" and become an expression of its highest power in every way. You will inspire through art and music. You will tell jokes, laugh, sing and dance. You will travel the world, cosmos and learn about every way that presents itself. You will teach by telling stories. You will gain as much knowledge as possible and you will give it back to as many people as possible. You will lead by example and be craved and worshipped by all. You will find meaning and have purpose.

#9 YOU WILL HEAL

You will understand that sleeping is a sacred act that allows you to sit with the gods until you are able to enter states that allow you to fully charge and heal without it. You will not be disturbed when doing so. You will sleep every night until you are fully rested and healed. You will spend much time in nature, grounding and getting fresh air. You will be charged by the sun. You will learn from the bird's chirps and the sounds from the wind and water. You will grow and prepare your own food with love and only drink the purest water. Everything you put in you will be medicine. You will appreciate the change of the seasons and all of the elements. You will spend much time at the mountaintops in stillness and silence. You will walk into rooms and heal everyone in them. You will induce awakenings in everyone you make contact with.

#10 YOU WILL DEMAND THAT OTHERS FOLLOW THESE RULES

You will not entertain lies or people's ideas of being broken, weak and anything less than all-powerful and all-capable. You will understand that we are one. You will understand that evil is ignorance. You will not be an enabler. You will understand that you are breaking these laws by allowing others to break them.

AFTERWORD

"Darkness is no longer welcome here."
- Master Nick Eagle

I hope you thoroughly enjoyed this book and have much appreciation for all of the energy and effort I put into it. I hope you have a new outlook on life and a new energy about you. I hope you look to leave behind fear and find truth. I hope you join me. I hope to meet you. I hope you awaken to your potential.

I am always open to taking on students. If you are called, please reach out on social media and you can find the links at my website nickeaglemystic.com

I am building a beautiful community and I will have beautiful gatherings at Eagle Vortex Awakening Sanctuary. I hope you stay with me and have the opportunity for one-on-one time here. I offer a variety of private retreat packages. More info at eaglevortex.com

I will travel the world as a maestro and curandero, hosting retreats and ceremonies and offering enlightening plants. If plants call to you, I should be your guide. Message me where to begin and request to be added to my private retreat list.

If the *Golden Laws of Enlightenment* touched you, please pass it on to all who are open to receiving them; deserving hands, of course.

Now, it's time for me to assemble a beautiful, high-vibrational album of song circle songs, chants, and healing sounds that you can meditate with, sing and play along to, as well as complete writing "How to Battle Darkness."

My Website for Awakening Sessions, my Enlightenment Protocol and Enlightenment Blog: nickeaglemystic.com

Eagle Vortex Awakening Sanctuary: eaglevortex.com

Inquiries: eagleawakenme@gmail.com

MASTER NICK EAGLE PHD

DEDICATED TO KAREN THE KADOMA

You were right, and I will not let another down

In Costa Rica just after it happened:

I have only just begun to heal the world

Take my hand so one day soon you will not need one

Learn what we are

I have not told you everything I have done and
everything that I know...